MOVIE GUIDE FOR LEGAL STUDIES

SECOND EDITION

KENT D. KAUFFMAN, ESQ.

Prentice Hall

Boston Columbus Indianapolis New York San Francisco Upper Saddle River

Amsterdam Cape Town Dubai London Madrid Milan Munich Paris Montreal Toronto

Delhi Mexico City Sao Paulo Sydney Hong Kong Seoul Singapore Taipei Tokyo

Editor in Chief: Vernon Anthony
Acquisitions Editor: Gary Bauer
Editorial Assistant: Megan Heintz
Director of Marketing: David Gesell
Marketing Manager: Leigh Ann Sims
Marketing Coordinator: Alicia Wozniak
Marketing Assistant: Les Roberts
Senior Managing Editor: JoEllen Gohr
Project Manager: Christina Taylor

Operations Specialist: Desidra Skahill
Art Director: Jayne Conte
Cover Art: Corbis
Cover Designer: Bruce Kenselaar
Copyeditor: Naomi Sysak
Printer/Binder: Bind-Rite Graphics / Robbinsville
Cover Printer: Lehigh-Phoenix Color/Hagerstown
Text Font: Times New Roman

10 9 8 7 6 5 4 3 2

Prentice Hall
is an imprint of

www.pearsonhighered.com

ISBN 10:   0-13-506375-2
ISBN 13: 978-0-13-506375-0

About the Author

Kent Kauffman is Assistant Professor of Business Law at Indiana University-Purdue University, Fort Wayne. He is a graduate of Temple University and The Dickinson School of Law of the Pennsylvania State University. Mr. Kauffman is the author of *Legal Ethics*, 2nd Ed., a textbook published by Cengage Learning. He is a recipient of Who's Who in American Law, Who's Who in American Education, and a multiple recipient of Who's Who Among America's Teachers.

Acknowledgments

This second edition would not be possible without the support of Gary Bauer, Senior Acquisition Editor at Prentice-Hall/Pearson Higher Education. It is always a pleasure to work with him and his team, including Linda Cupp, Developmental Editor, and Megan Heintz, Editorial Assistant. And as with any venture I undertake, nothing would ever be gained without the abiding encouragement and patience of my wife, Karen.

CONTENTS

INTRODUCTION

Some might say that giving a movie guide to a college professor is like giving an Atlas to an agoraphobic: Just because it's free doesn't make it useful. But I prefer to think of it as giving a painting kit to an inventor: Just because it isn't empirical doesn't mean it won't inspire. And, inspiration is a resource that professors and inventors need in large supply.

In the past decade, I have come to realize that students almost expect to be entertained in the classroom. As more and more students take classes between coming and going to work and raising children, they seem to distract and tire more easily. Lectures that used to take shape in the presentation of ideas and facts supplemented by a chalkboard, gave way to PowerPoint presentations and Internet connections. Where once good instructors sought to keep their lectures fresh, they now feel pressure to make them novel, and strong visual aids promote novelty.

Furthermore, students benefit from movies, and I was no different. I can remember as a freshman watching *Gandhi* in Intellectual Heritage, and as a sophomore watching *Ordinary People* in Interpersonal Communication. Both viewings were valuable learning experiences, especially since the professors discussed the films afterwards. And legal students love legal movies. They love them not because legal movies are technically accurate (for that is almost irrelevant) but because they portray the basics of American life—good and evil, guilt and innocence, death, justice, rights, freedom, and money—in the context of the legal system, which has quite an allure in film. Documentaries are tremendous teaching aids and can be quite interesting, but they almost always need to be shown in their entirety. Movies are also easier to find and bring to class, especially for the adjunct instructor whose out-of-class time is woefully compensated.

The purposes of this guide are multifold. Naturally, it is intended to help you incorporate one or more of these films into your classes. By providing a summary of the plot and types of classes for which one of the listed films might fit, you can choose whether you want to find the movie in your local rental store or public library and preview it for class use, especially if it is one you've never seen. Or, in conjunction with the key scene and discussion suggestion portions, you can provide your students with sufficient narrative, and rather than show a movie in its entirety, show one or more of its key scenes, incorporating those scenes into your class material and dialogue. I have used the key-scene-only method with *A Civil Action*, *Class Action*, *Changing Lanes*, *Wall Street*, and *The Verdict*. Beyond classroom viewing, you might use this guide when creating class projects by having students watch an assigned movie and then apply it in a research paper (or some other legal writing task) to their course material or jurisdiction's law. That has worked well for me with *The Rainmaker* and *Erin Brockovich*.

Do the legal scenes in some of these movies strain credulity? Sure. They are, after all, fiction. But that's where you come in, to provide analysis and perspective. Furthermore, dissecting a scene's inaccuracies can be illuminating and amusing.

The second edition has a few features that will, hopefully, make this a more valuable tool and easier to use. Two new sections have been added. The first provides a walk-through on finding legal movies at three film Web sites that have excellent search tools. If by the end of this book you haven't found a movie that might work for your class, you can look for it on the same Web sites I've scoured. This guide, even in its second edition, has several omissions, a few by intention. Sorry *Body of Evidence* and *Legally Blond*e (both of you). Please feel free to contact me if you think additions should be made; I haven't seen them all.

The second addition to this edition is a small summary of the copyright law and its application to showing movie clips and complete films in your classes. Suffice it to say that unless you're selling seat licenses or charging tickets for your classes, or you teach at an unaccredited, for-profit college, there is nothing to worry about.

New movies have been added to the second edition, although not all the movies are, in the historical sense, new (*The Paper Chase*). The "key scene" and corresponding "discussion suggestion" paragraphs have been placed inside text borders to make finding each key scene a bit easier. If using this compendium helps make your classroom experiences more rewarding, then I'm happy. If reading it is enjoyable, then I'm especially happy.

FINDING YOUR OWN LEGAL MOVIES

After looking through all the movie listings that follow, you might think to yourself, "Why isn't that one listed? He missed a good one." Well, you're right. I most likely did overlook a legal film that would have been ideal for a key scene showing in your legal class. The bad news is I either made a mistake in choosing not to put in a legal film that I found lacking for this movie guide (*Legally Blonde*, for one), or I failed to watch a worthy entrant that would have made your legal class all the more enriching. The good news is that I can show you how to be your own celluloid sleuth. Although not nearly as pinpoint accurate as conducting legal research on Westlaw® or Lexis®, using the search features of a few excellent movie Web sites can help you find more legal movies that might have the key scenes you're looking for. While the number of movie-based Web sites is voluminous, three in particular will likely be sufficient: All Movie, The Internet Movie Database, and Rotten Tomatoes.

AllMovie.com

AllMovie (www.allmovie.com) is my favorite film-search Web site and is part of the All Media Guide of related Web sites. At one time referred to as "All Movie Guide," this Web site has what I think is the most layered search mechanism.

The starting point on allmovie.com is the search bar at the top of the opening screen. After entering a legal film into the search bar, a list of all the movies with the same name (or similar names) will appear. By clicking on the film title you want, you'll be provided with a plot synopsis and tabs for finding more information on your film, such as user reviews. Below the synopsis will be a list of movies under a heading entitled "Similar Works." For example, the page for the Paul Newman film *The Verdict* includes 10 other related movies, including a few that were included in the first edition of *Movie Guide for Legal Studies*, and one (*Absence of Malice*, also starring Paul Newman) that is included in the second edition. All the movies placed under the Similar Works heading are hyperlinked, so clicking on any of them—such as *Criminal*

Lawyer (1951), also listed for *The Verdict*—brings up a new page—which of course would have its own Similar Works enumeration.

The best feature on allmovie.com is that for each movie search the reader is also given a variety of related search links that descend on the left side of the Web page, underneath a photograph for the film. Categories such as "Genre," "Types," Keywords," "Themes," and "Tones," provide more hyperlinks that lead to more movies. Continuing with the example of *The Verdict*, underneath the category of Types is listed "courtroom drama." By clicking on that, the reader is given a new Web page that summarizes what constitutes a courtroom drama movie, with suggested titles, and then a full list of movies that fit the courtroom drama theme. As of this writing, there were 64 movies listed, from *Amistad* to *Young Mr. Lincoln*, each one hyperlinked.

Back on the main page for *The Verdict*, one of the words listed under the category of Keywords is "lawyer." By clicking on that tag, you will be brought to a new page with hundreds of movies listed that can be directly accessed. By clicking on "fighting the system" under Themes, there are dozens of movies listed, including *Norma Rae* and *Office Space*, two excellent movies with different approaches to an us-against-them-at-work narrative, each one with key scenes that could be used in a labor relations or corporations class. If your students haven't had a Lumbergh for a boss (or a red stapler), showing them a scene from *Office Space* might help you discuss the doctrine of at-will employment, or adequate provocation killings. After spending a few minutes on allmovie.com, you'll blissfully forget that there is more to preparing for class than prospecting for movies.

The Internet Movie Database

The Internet Movie Database (www.imdb.com) is a veritable goldmine of all things movie related. A Web site for hardcore movie enthusiasts, this clearing house of movie information will tell you everything you could ever want to know about any movie ever made, which might even include your family holiday home-movies. It also has some terrific search mechanisms that allow you to find your own legal films.

The home screen for imdb.com includes a search bar near the top, and by entering a film title you'll be brought to the Web page for that film. There you will find links to all kinds of jumping off points for more information, from director and writer to the cast, to plot lines and tag lines, to user comments. Running down the left side of your film's Web page are hyperlinks to even more information on the film, including trivia and errors. For instance, by choosing *The Rainmaker*, you'll be able to find trivia, such as this is John Grisham's favorite film adaptation of his novels, and that Edward Norton tried out for the role of Rudy Baylor. The folks at imdb.com take finding film goofs so seriously that of the 15 errors they found for *The Rainmaker*, one is of the infamous "stupid, stupid, stupid" letter Great Benefit Insurance sends leukemia sufferer Donny Ray. According to Rudy Baylor, the letter is signed by company vice president Everett Lufkin, but in the same scene it is shown to be signed by senior claims supervisor Russell Krokit.

Finding legal films on imdb.com is as easy as it is on allmovie.com. After choosing a legal film and getting to that film's Web page, you can link to other films through Web tags listed under the film's title, such as "Genre" and "Plot Keywords." Near the bottom of the page are

"Recommendations," movies that imdb.com thinks you might want to investigate based on your primary search. The last part of the Recommendations portion is a "Show More Recommendations" link, and by clicking on that you'll get an expanded list of recommended films. For *The Rainmaker*, the Recommendations include five films (all included in this book), but the Show More Recommendations link leads to five other movies, including *The Devil's Advocate* (not included in this book).

Similar to the appearance on allmovie.com, there is a vertical column on the left side of your chosen movie's Web page that has various Web tags for movie research, including a "Quick Links" bar that allows the reader to access more information than initially provided by the left-column tags. When clicking on the "keywords" Quick Links for *The Rainmaker*, 18 keyword hyperlinks are provided. After clicking on one of them—jury—you will be given at least 218 related legal movies or television shows, listed in order of their average imdb.com user rating. *12 Angry Men* appears first. Also on the same page is a large box on the right side, which is a keyword refiner that has hundreds of words inside, allowing you to add key word tags to your original refiner and conduct a metasearch. With all of the search refiners imdb.com provides, one would think no movie would be missed. Alas, when I entered a refiner search with the keywords of "evidence," "father daughter relationships," and "jury," *Class Action* was excluded from the results, even though it is about two lawyers, a father and a daughter, opposing each other in a huge civil suit.

Rotten Tomatoes

Rotten Tomatoes (www.rottentomatoes.com) is the best Web site for learning about movies without having to actually watch them. Although this purveyor of movie reviews does more than just allow you to find and read hundreds of movie reviews for thousands of movies, the other attributes of Rotten Tomatoes—such as listing current movie and DVD rankings, movie times in your area and providing celebrity interviews—pale in comparison in its primary objective. All the reviews for any chosen film are averaged for the Web site's "tomatometer," and if at least 60 percent of all the reviews are positive, the movie will be listed as "fresh." Anything less and the movie is—you guessed it—"rotten."

If you are considering showing a film you've never seen and it is not included in this book—*The Music Box* (1989), for instance—search for it on Rotten Tomatoes' primary search tool located near the top of the opening Web page, and you'll be taken to a list of movies with that title or similar titles. Clicking on the correct version of *The Music Box* will get you to a new page where 14 reviews are provided, not all of them still accessible. *Find Me Guilty* (2006), a much more recent legal film, has 99 available reviews. By reading reviews from esteemed reviewers like Roger Ebert or online-only reviewers like James Berardinelli, one can learn quite a lot about a film's plot and subplot, key characters, and conflicts. You don't have to go to the video store or order the movie through Amazon.com, and then set aside an afternoon or evening to see if the film might contain any classroom-appropriate key scenes.

Rotten Tomatoes also has its own specialized search feature, "Tomato Picker," although it's initially titled as "Browse Movies" on the opening Web page of any selected movie. Tomato Picker's initial specialized search feature is rudimentary compared to allmovie.com and imdb.com, but after getting into it, the second layer of Tomato Picker allows you to choose movies by subgenre, including legal movies, as well as by tomatometer, MPAA rating, and decade of release. After winnowing your search to specified fields, you'll be given many movies, which could take a bit of time to peruse. But having too many possibilities from which to choose is better than the alternative, and Rotten Tomatoes can be a valuable tool for your legal movie treasure hunt.

COPYRIGHT LAW AND YOUR CLASSROOM

Some years ago, while at a college where I no longer work, I was in the section of the library where faculty search for library-owned videos and DVDs. After a fruitless rummage through the stacks to find a legal movie I thought the library owned, I asked the librarian where it might be. She said the library didn't own the film, but that I could put forward a request to have the library order a copy. At this college, "request" was code for filling out four requisition documents, getting three supervisors' signatures, making two budget reviews…and a partridge in a pear tree. I told her I'd just rent the thing myself and bring it to class. You would have thought I suggested book burning as a way to keep the classrooms warm in winter.

Such is the reaction of the gatekeepers of intellectual property. One can't fault her for doing her job—believing that only a library-owned and licensed DVD could be shown in class—regardless of her white-knuckled insistence. The fear of copyright infringement and its attendant liability is both legitimate and, depending on the circumstances, unfounded. The problem with knowing which description applies to our fear is that often those who tell us about infringement are administrators or librarians, who usually get their information from a seminar or a law class they took when getting a master's degree. So, in case you're ever confronted as I was, I thought it might be appropriate for this edition of *Movie Guide for Legal Studies* to provide a primer in what the copyright statutes say about the use of movie clips, or even movies, in a classroom setting.

Copyright protection flows from the U.S. Constitution, which grants exclusive legislative power to the U.S. Congress. In 2002, key copyright statutes were amended, most noticeably with the addition of what is known as the Technology, Education and Copyright Harmonization Act (the TEACH Act, 17 U.S.C. § 110). While the focus on the TEACH Act was modernizing the copyright laws with respect to distance learning environments, part of the benefits concern the showing of copyrighted audio-visual works.

Face-to-face teaching environments are covered in 17 U.S.C. § 110(1) and, summarily, the law exempts the showing of entire movies from being an infringement. In order for the display to be lawful, the following factors must apply:

> the showing must be part of a teaching activity
> a teacher or pupil must be showing it
> the college or university must be nonprofit
> the showing must be in a classroom or similar place devoted to instruction

These qualifications result in the display being considered private, and it is private showings of movies that are noninfringing. Therefore, if you are teaching a class at a nonprofit institution, you may not only show any of the key scenes described in this book, you may show the whole movie, provided—according to the statute—the copy of the film you are showing is a lawfully authorized copy. So, if a student hands you an odd-looking DVD of *Michael Clayton*, which happens also to have "2008 high school graduation" written in Sharpie marker on the top-side, walk away slowly.

Distance learning education is covered in Section 110(2). There is a tighter rein put on the showing of movies in this statute, in light of the fact that distance learning courses can, theoretically, be held anywhere and everywhere and be transmitted to an almost limitless audience. The first key difference between face-to-face and distance-learning showings of films is that Section 110(2) allows for the "performance of…reasonable and limited portions…." Consequentially, unlike traditional educational settings, distance-learning colleges are only allowed to show movie clips. Not to worry: Movie clips are the objective of *Movie Guide for Legal Studies*. Another important distinction is that the instructor showing the movie clip must be teaching at a distance learning institution that is an "accredited," nonprofit institution [17 U.S.C. § 110(2)(A)]. In contrast, the portion of the statute on face-to-face instruction only requires that the college or university be nonprofit. Furthermore, the performance must be made only to enrolled students in the course, and the institution at where the film scene is shown must distribute written policies on copyright law compliance [17 U.S.C. § 110(2)(C) and (D)]. By following the requirements of the TEACH Act, those who teach in a distance learning institution will still be able to lawfully show key film scenes. And, of course, assigning students to watch a movie or a key film scene on their own is not an infringement.

Without the express coverage of 17 U.S.C § 110, instructors could still rely upon the Fair Use Doctrine as a safe harbor for the showing of film scenes in their classes. Located in 17 U.S.C. § 107, the fair use statute allows for the noninfringement use of copyrighted materials, when the use is for named purposes, including "teaching." Be advised: The use of copyrighted materials isn't considered fair just because one is using them in a teaching capacity. The statute provides four factors that determine if any given use is, in fact, fair. They are the following: the purpose and character of the copyrighted work (i.e., commercial versus educational use); the nature of the copyrighted work; the amount used in comparison to the copyrighted work in whole; and the effect the use would have on the potential market or value of the copyrighted work [17 U.S.C. § 107(1)-(4)]. Despite the lack of consistent precedent interpreting the four factors of fair use, I think that showing a film scene or two from any given film in a college classroom setting for the purposes of amplifying one's teaching, would be reasonable and fair.

12 ANGRY MEN (NR; 1957)

Key Themes: Jury deliberations, reasonable doubt, prejudice versus fairness
Best Classroom Use: Criminal Law, Introduction to Paralegal Studies

95 minutes
Cast: Henry Fonda, Lee J. Cobb, Ed Begley, Sr., Jack Warden, Jack Klugman,
             E.G. Marshall

12 Angry Men is so perfect for classroom viewing, it would almost be a shame to only show certain key scenes, especially since this movie is a play put on film, where later scenes depend on earlier ones. This character study of 12 jurors deliberating the murder case of a young Puerto Rican man prosecuted for murdering his father is highly entertaining and instructive. Without any of the typical action scenes so identified with today's legal thrillers, this movie's focus on thought provoking dialogue about challenging the prejudices and assumptions brought into the jury room makes for a more rewarding experience. Long considered a classic, *12 Angry Men* might yet be unknown to many students who would benefit from seeing it.

A trial judge listlessly tells a 12-man jury that the fate—and life—of a young man is in their hands. If they find him guilty of premeditated murder, the sentence will have to be death. So, off they file into the steamy jury room to deliberate on the evidence. But deliberation seems to be a matter of semantics for these men who are dismissive of the very idea, and are ready to leave as soon as their work is to begin. That is, until Juror No. 8 (Henry Fonda) votes not guilty in the initial tally, annoying some of the others, including the prejudiced Juror No. 10 (Ed Begley); the angry and bitter Juror No. 3 (Lee J. Cobb); the deductive Juror No. 4 (E.G. Marshall); and the carefree Juror No. 7 (Jack Warden), whose guilty vote is based more on his desire to use the Yankees tickets burning a hole in his pocket. The other jurors, like much of society, acquiesce to the dominant men, or simply figure that anyone who has been arrested, charged, and prosecuted with the use of eyewitness testimony must be guilty.

Henry Fonda gets the other jurors to consent to at least discussing the case for one hour, and they proceed, one after another, to tell him why they think the defendant is guilty. Some of the jurors are convinced by the eyewitness testimony of two neighbors, one who claimed to hear, and the other to see, the murder. Others are satisfied by the motive for the murder—the son's evident hatred for his father, evidenced by a witness who heard the son yell, "I'm gonna kill you!" Some of the jurors believe the timeline and the defendant's flimsy alibi, combined with the physical evidence of the rare switchblade used in the killing, lead to guilty being the logical verdict. And still others think that the defendant's violent past, combined with the "natural tendencies of those types" of slum dwellers, make it easy to give a death sentence. Fonda brilliantly combats that prejudice by avoiding it directly, instead tackling the other jurors' notions about the evidence with an approach as methodical as the architect he is, and with a bit of Clarence Darrow-styled sleight of hand. Finally, when most of the others have changed their verdicts, the last holdouts can only cling to their bigotry and bitterness. Throughout the film, Fonda's character never insists the defendant didn't do it; he asks the jurors to consider that it's possible the evidence isn't all that it seemed to be. By the film's end, reasonable doubt has been found, which doesn't necessarily mean an innocent man has been freed.

Key Scene—As if bored, the trial judge unenthusiastically instructs the jury in the film's opening scene. He tells the jurors that the defendant has been charged with first-degree murder and will be sentenced to death if they find him guilty.

Discussion Suggestion—Discuss how in today's legal system the guilt phase is separate from the penalty phase. You could discuss the U.S. Supreme Court case, *Blakely v. Washington*, 542 U.S. 296 (2004), which held that judges may not make exceptional sentencing enhancements based on evidence not submitted to a jury and proven beyond a reasonable doubt. Research your jurisdiction's criminal code to see if any crime beyond first-degree murder is death penalty eligible, and examine their death penalty statute to see under what circumstances (i.e., aggravating and mitigating circumstances) a death sentence may be given.

Key Scene—Juror No. 4 (E.G. Marshall) is a stockbroker who applies logic and deductive reasoning when it is his turn to tell Henry Fonda why the defendant is guilty. He focuses on the timing of the events on the night of the murder, the eyewitness testimony, and the fact that the murder weapon, a switchblade knife, just happened to be the exact type of knife the defendant owned, but claimed fell out of his pocket on the night of the murder. Fonda suggests that someone else with the same knife could have committed the murder, but the stockbroker replies how impossible that would be, since the knife in question was so rare. With that, Fonda stands up and pulls from his jacket pocket a switchblade that is identical to the one in evidence sticking out of the jury room table, telling the men that he bought it at a pawn shop in the defendant's neighborhood the night before.

Discussion Suggestion—Can jurors do this kind of thing? Although it makes for a great scene, any juror who engages in such sleuthing will be in serious trouble, as will the entire case. Since Henry Fonda's character helped raise reasonable doubt in such a dubious way, then should we consider whether he was as close-minded about the evidence as were the other jurors at the start of the deliberation?

THE ACCUSED (R; 1988)

Key Themes: Sexual assault and justice, plea bargaining, guilt by encouragement
Best Classroom Use: Criminal Law, Interviewing

110 minutes   (graphic rape scene and nudity, strong language)
Cast: Jodie Foster, Kelly McGillis, Bernie Coulson, Leo Rossi, Ann Hearn

Based loosely on a gang rape committed in 1983 in New Bedford, Massachusetts, *The Accused* is a strong film with a rape scene in it that is so hard to watch it might be too graphic for classroom viewing. However, the key scenes can still be presented without having to show the film in its entirety.

Jodi Foster won an Oscar for Best Actress playing Sarah Tobias, a young woman who is brutalized in the backroom of a seedy bar late one evening. Having gone to the bar after a fight with her boyfriend, Sarah begins drinking and smoking pot. Soon, she is flirting and playing pinball with a few guys who eventually brutalize her. Although the rape is shown toward the end of the movie in a flashback, there is no doubt from the beginning that she was the victim of a vicious crime, and that it was watched like a sporting event, with cheering spectators. As assistant prosecutor Kathryn Murphy (Kelly McGillis) comes to the hospital to interview Sarah, Kathryn casts a dim view toward her victim for reasons that come to fruition: There are no witnesses who will come forward to verify Sarah's version of events, and Sarah is poor white trash with a checkered past who was drunk and taking drugs that night.

Three men, including one fraternity brother, are arrested and charged, but it becomes evident that the case has some weaknesses that the defense will pounce on at trial. Kathryn and her boss are not too thrilled with their chances at trial and strike a plea bargain with the three defendants. The men will plead guilty to reckless endangerment, an offense with no sexual connotation, and serve a few months behind bars. Sarah learns of this plea bargain while watching the news, confirming her belief that no one is on her side. Eventually, Sarah's act of rage against a guy in the bar that night, who cruelly taunts her about what happened, lands her in the hospital, broken again. And Kathryn's guilt over the cheap plea bargain she struck leads her once more to file criminal charges against those involved in the rapes.

At this point, *The Accused* takes a most interesting turn. Kathryn's legal strategy is to now charge the men who gleefully hooted and hollered during the multiple rapes with the crime of solicitation—that they feloniously encouraged or induced the rapists to act. Her two most important witnesses are Sarah, who, considering her condition during the attack, has difficulty identifying these goading onlookers, and Kenneth Joyce (Bernie Coulson), a fraternity brother of one of the rapists who also saw the rape and anonymously called 911, but who is having second thoughts about his involvement in the trial. It is during Kenneth's testimony that we finally see the brutality of the rapists and the brazenness of those who were much more than onlookers.

Key Scene—There is a short scene where Kathryn goes to the bar where the rape occurred and interviews Sarah's friend Sally, who worked that night and with whom Sarah had spent some time before going to the backroom to play pinball with one of the attackers. Although Sally believes Sarah's allegation, Sally didn't see anything clearly because the backroom was so crowded. When asked about identifying the witnesses who were blocking her view, Sally says she can't remember anything about them. Kathryn then asks a few clipped follow-up questions, which jog Sally's memory, causing her to remember that one of the guys had a scorpion tattoo on his arm. Later in the film, that tattoo will be critical to Kathryn's decision to charge some of the witnesses with solicitation.

Discussion Suggestion—Discuss how interviewers need to listen carefully to what an interviewee is saying, and how trying different approaches and follow-up questions can lead to key pieces of information.

Key Scene—Kathryn visits Sarah at her trailer a few days after the rape and begins to sternly question Sarah about how much she had to drink that night, how provocatively dressed Sarah was when she went to the bar, about her sexual proclivities and disease history, and about her criminal record. Sarah is insulted by such an inquisition, but Kathryn tells her that these types of questions are only the beginning of what Sarah will face as the case proceeds.

Discussion Suggestion—First, do a little Internet research on the Kobe Bryant rape case from Colorado in 2003, which ended in the charges being dropped. In light of Kobe Bryant's lawyers' tactics during that short-lived sexual assault prosecution, discuss how your jurisdiction's rape shield law would apply to Sarah's personal history.

Key Scene—Feeling guilt-ridden over her treatment of Sarah and her case, Kathryn does some late night legal research and the next morning explains to her boss, the district attorney, how she is planning on charging some of the witnesses to the rape with solicitation, namely that they encouraged and induced the rapists to act through their goading and cheering. Her boss thinks that it is ludicrous to attempt to apply the solicitation statute to these onlookers, and her insistence leads to a permanent break in their relationship.

Discussion Suggestion—After examining your own jurisdiction's solicitation statute, analyze whether Kathryn's theory holds water. Does cheering at and offering colored commentary to a vicious crime make those witnesses guilty of any crime, much less solicitation?

ANATOMY OF A MURDER (NR; 1959)

Key Themes: Insanity defense, heat of passion killing, questionable legal strategies, domestic violence
Best Classroom Use: Criminal Law, Legal Ethics, Interviewing

161 minutes   (explicit sexual discussions)
Cast: Jimmy Stewart, Lee Remick, Ben Gazzara, Arthur O'Connell, Eve Arden, George C. Scott, Joseph Welch

Decades before Scott Turow and John Grisham wrote best-selling legal thrillers that morphed into films, Michigan Supreme Court Justice John D. Voelker, using the pen name Robert Traver, wrote the novel, *Anatomy of a Murder*, which was turned into a film one year later. This superb film shot on location in the Upper Peninsula of Michigan, was nominated for a Best Picture Oscar and was years ahead of its time, in both the subject matter and the way with which the subject is dealt.

Jimmy Stewart stars as Paul Biegler, a defense lawyer in a small town in Michigan's Upper Peninsula who recently lost his reelection as district attorney. Paul Biegler's new office is his home—literally. As the movie unfolds, Paul is asked to represent an army lieutenant accused of murdering the owner of a local bar. The initial interview of Lieutenant Manion (Ben Gazzara) shows a tension between a lawyer who is more comfortable prosecuting guys who kill people, and a defendant who is so conceited he asks Biegler about Biegler's legal experience. And here is where the movie begins its controversial path. Manion claims he shot and killed Mr. Quill, the bar owner, because Quill raped Manion's wife (Lee Remick) on that night. Because of the hour-long difference between Manion's awareness of the rape and his action, Biegler tells Manion there is no justification defense available to him. As the interview progresses, Biegler helps Manion realize that his defense should be insanity, in that he was so angry his wife was raped by Quill that he had an irresistible impulse to kill Quill, which he did by shooting Quill five times in the bar. And so proceeds what might be a dishonest defense.

When Biegler interviews Manion's wife, we are unsure whether she was raped or not because as she tells him of how Quill attacked her in his car while driving her home from the bar, her story doesn't seem to cohere. And she is flirting with Biegler within minutes of meeting him. As Biegler tries to prepare for a high profile trial on behalf of a client he doesn't really like, whose defense is one that Biegler doesn't really believe, a few plot twists are provided for good measure.

The movie's trial scenes are quite enjoyable and lengthy, with direct and cross-examinations of key witnesses that are given the time needed to be developed. Jimmy Stewart's small-town persona is a dodge: He outwits the prosecution at every turn, using sanctimony, sarcasm, and humor in front of the jury, and in chambers uses century-old case law on the allowance of irresistible impulse. He puts the dead victim on trial, often over the protest of the prosecution and rebuke of the trial judge. During key parts of the trial, the lawyers use words like sperm and panties, a notable choice of frank language for a film of that era. The issue of insanity in *Anatomy of a Murder* is handled in ways that seem fit for today's theatrical legal dramas. We know that Lieutenant Manion knew right from wrong on the night he killed Quill, but the standard of irresistible impulse (quite different from the historical M'Naughten rule) leaves room to debate notions of self-control and personal responsibility.

Key Scene—The initial interview between Biegler and Manion (Ben Gazzara) shows a lawyer helping his client figure out that he should say he was insane at the time of the killing. The client interview is prematurely cut short, and while Jimmy Stewart eats lunch with his alcoholic lawyer friend, the friend helps Stewart realize that it is the defense lawyer's job to find a suitable, even manufactured, defense for such a client. So Stewart goes back to the jail and tells Manion that there are four kinds of defenses to a charge of murder: accident or suicide, alibi, justification, or excuse. Stewart tells Manion the only defense that might apply is excuse. It is from there that Manion begins to come to the realization that he was insane.

Discussion Suggestion—Upon watching this scene, discuss whether the insanity defense is actually appropriate for Lieutenant Manion, and whether Paul Biegler's conduct is ethical.

Key Scene—During the defense's evidence phase, an army psychiatrist testifies about what he previously determined from examining Manion. His conclusion is that Manion suffered from a dissociative reaction brought on by his wife's announcement that Quill raped her, which caused him to suffer from an irresistible impulse to kill Quill.

Discussion Suggestion—This scene would be useful for a discussion on the specifics of the insanity defense, including the rare standard of irresistible impulse. But even more so, the scene would be helpful for a discussion on voluntary manslaughter, which is the defense that jumps out at the viewer within the first 15 minutes of the movie. When one thinks about what voluntary manslaughter really is, it seems to be an impulse reaction that is irresistible, particularly when thought of in its paramour context. Also, debate the pros and cons of having a voluntary manslaughter defense that seems more lenient than its insanity counterpart, at least in many jurisdictions.

...AND JUSTICE FOR ALL. (R; 1979)

Key Themes: Corruption in the legal system, injustice, judicial misbehavior, ethical dilemmas

Best Classroom Use: Introduction to Paralegal Studies, Criminal Procedure, Legal Ethics

120 minutes: (violence, strong language, nudity)
Cast: Al Pacino, Jack Warden, John Forsythe, Christine Lahti, Jeffrey Tambor

Rarely has a movie presented a bleaker picture of a corrupt and decrepit legal system. Although *And Justice for All* received its share of criticism from the legal community when it was released, this satire is prophetic in a way, presaging a public's ever-increasing animosity towards lawyers and the justice system, as well portraying one man's fight against injustice and cronyism years before Turow, Grisham, or Martini. There is much to discuss from this film, although little to find uplifting, other than the most viscerally satisfying opening statement ever put on film.

Arthur Kirkland (Al Pacino) is a Baltimore defense lawyer with a motley crew of clients, including a drag queen charged with robbery, an illegal lottery runner eating the evidence in court, and a poor young man trying for over a year to get out of jail after being wrongfully convicted because a computer error mistook him for someone else with the same name. Even Kirkland, himself, has been jailed for contempt-of-court-quality dealings with Judge Henry T. Fleming (John Forsythe), who arrogantly refused to consider Kirkland's plea for reconsideration of the evidence that the young man has been wrongfully convicted. If that isn't enough, Arthur's law partner (Jeffrey Tambor) is coming apart at the seams more and more each day, and Kirkland is under scrutiny by the legal ethics committee, which has decided it's time to clean up the corruption, making every lawyer a subject of its investigation. But the ethics committee is more corrupt than its targets, and Arthur's personal involvement with one of the committee members (Christine Lahti) does nothing to get the investigatory light shed on the judges, one of whom, Fleming, is a self-righteous autocrat, and another who has a penchant for attempting suicide in between court recesses.

Arthur Kirkland's concern for his clients' well-being is deep and rare in this justice system where defendants are handled and tossed away by their lawyers like tissues. But when Judge Fleming is arrested and charged with rape, the lawyer he wants to represent him is the one we'd least suspect. Naturally, Arthur wants nothing less than to represent his sanctimonious enemy, but he is threatened with a disbarment proceeding related to a long-ago breach of confidentiality controversy if he doesn't succumb. Arthur hopes that by representing Fleming, the judge will finally move on those repeated motions to reconsider the evidence for his wrongfully imprisoned client, who is becoming more vulnerable and desperate by the day. While trying to deal with his partner's loss of sanity, and clients who are begging to be let out of jail, Kirkland is building a defense for the smug and politically connected Judge Fleming. When Kirkland learns the indisputable proof of Fleming's guilt in the sadistic crime, he faces the mother of all dilemmas. How he handles it is a career killer, but worth the sacrifice.

Key Scene—Unexpectedly late one evening, Arthur Kirkland's law partner, Jay Porter (Jeffrey Tambor), knocks on Kirkland's apartment door. He is long past drunk and his ramblings begin to make sense as he reminds Kirkland of a past murder client that he, Porter, was able to get off on a "technicality." As Porter's voice grows louder and more pained, he tells Kirkland that his former client has just killed two children. Soon, Porter will have a complete breakdown in the courthouse.

Discussion Suggestion—Although lawyers are paid to use every procedural advantage available and are not considered blameworthy for getting their clients off on "technicalities," much of the public might disagree. Discuss whether Porter should bear any responsibility for his former client's actions. They might even indicate whether any of them would be opposed to working for a criminal defense lawyer because of some of the issues shown in that scene.

Key Scene—After a near-death experience in a helicopter with the judge with suicidal tendencies, Kirkland is asked by the judge about the Fleming case. After Kirkland tells that judge about his refusal to take Fleming's case, the judge glibly warns Kirkland that he had better reconsider, or else the ethics committee will seek to have him disbarred. Shocked, Kirkland asks what he could be disbarred for, and the judge mentions that Kirkland allegedly breached the confidentiality of a former client. Kirkland tells his side of the story: His former burglary client was a crazy scumbag who often talked about putting a lit firecracker in someone's mouth, and when Kirkland read in the newspaper about such a crime occurring, he reported what he knew to the police, which helped catch that guy. Despite his belief in the rightness of his actions, Kirkland is forced to take Fleming's case.

Discussion Suggestion—There is a lot going on in this scene. Were Kirkland's actions a breach of confidentiality? Were his burglary client's rantings about wanting to do sadistic things to others covered by the duty of confidentiality or the attorney-client privilege? If they are, can Kirkland ethically breach his confidentiality duty under the client criminality exception? What if a paralegal was in Kirkland's position and heard those threatening statements? Would he or she be allowed to do what Kirkland did, assuming he wasn't wrong?

Key Scene—After Judge Fleming passes a lie detector test concerning the rape charge, one of Kirkland's long-standing clients gives him Polaroid pictures of Fleming and the Chair of the Ethics Panel with the prostitute, and dressed in sadomasochistic outfits. Kirkland confronts Fleming in the law library with the pictures, and Fleming coolly admits his guilt and tells Kirkland to go back to work preparing the defense. Kirkland tells his girlfriend about the pictures, and she tells him that the pictures don't prove Fleming raped anyone.

Discussion Suggestion—Assuming the prosecution possessed those pictures, would they be admissible in your jurisdiction? Do some research and discuss this. Did Kirkland breach confidentiality by telling his girlfriend about the pictures?

Key Scene—The most famous scene in the movie shows the opening statements of Fleming's rape trial, with Kirkland beginning a seemingly favorable statement, even intentionally mentioning the passed polygraph test, over the trial judge's anger. And then, Kirkland turns on a dime, yelling and cursing and proclaiming Judge Fletcher's guilt. The bailiffs frantically pick Kirkland up and carry him out of court, even as Kirkland continues his harangue on the justice system.

Discussion Suggestion—Not much should be needed to get a discussion going on Kirkland's outburst and propriety. Should he be praised or punished for what he did?

ANIMAL FARM (NR; 1954)

Key Themes: Justice, freedom, government control, equality
Best Classroom Use: Constitutional Law, Introduction to Law

72 minutes   (violence, cruelty to animals)
Cast: Gordon Heath (the narrator), Maurice Denham (all the voices)

Sadly, it is unlikely that more than a handful of students in any college class today would have read *Animal Farm*, one of the most significant and exhortative novels of the 20th century. Although "Orwellian," "*1984*," and "Big Brother" have become buzzwords about totalitarian tactics, there can be no dystopian world of *1984* without *Animal Farm*. A book about talking farm animals can only be made into a cartoon film, and this version, supposedly financed by the CIA to be an artistic weapon of the cold war, is recommended over the TNT version made in 1999. To the dismay of some, the film version deviates from the novel, not only because it has some missing characters, but in its upbeat ending. Strictly speaking, this is not a legal movie. But, all legal systems are children of their political systems, and legal students should view this cautionary tale, lest they come to believe that legal rights and freedoms are immutable.

When Farmer Jones's neglectfulness of Manor Farm and drunken brutality against its animals become more than they can bear, a boar named Old Major holds a barn meeting, predicting the cruel endings of all the animals and imploring them to rise up and overthrow Farmer Jones's dominion. After successfully tossing out their master, the animals try to create their own utopia, adopting a revolutionary song, throwing out all the old human remnants of farm life, ridding themselves of class distinctions, and painting seven rules of Animal Farm life on the side of their barn. These famous rules include, "no beds," "four legs good, two legs bad," "no animal shall kill another," and "all animals are equal." But from almost the beginning of the revolution, things don't go as Old Major envisioned: fractures occur, political murders are committed, class distinctions return (with the pigs being the ruling class), conspiratorial accusations are manufactured to maintain control over the masses, and the animals' most sacred rule is amended to read, "All animals are equal, but some animals are more equal than others." Finally, the downtrodden animals muster up the courage for a second revolution, this time against the pigs and their Stalinist leader, Napoleon.

Key Scene—Old Major calls a secret meeting in the barn early in the film, and implores the animals to rise up and overthrow Farmer Jones. Using brilliant persuasive tactics, he describes the animals' present deprivations and predicts their future demise at the slaughterhouse or glue factory, once Farmer Jones stops viewing them as useful to him. Old Major's speech includes some of the mantras of traditional communism (George Orwell's ideology), encouraging the animals that if they would overthrow their tyrant, they would "be rich and free," and that "all animals are equal." Soon after, the revolution begins.

Discussion Suggestion—Consider whether a legal system can provide true equality and, if so, what does it mean to say that all of us are equal? Is Old Major meaning what Jefferson meant when he wrote, "All men are created equal…"?

Key Scene—Long after Napoleon has murdered Snowball, his chief rival, accusing him post-death of treason, Napoleon stages another show trial. This time, after violating the rule against taking a chicken's eggs, Napoleon demands to know who besides the chickens has been treasonous to the cause. As a result, a few animals are led away and murdered, which doesn't violate the "no animal shall kill another animal" rule since the rule has been amended to read, "No animal shall kill another animal without cause."

Discussion Suggestion—Discuss how language is used, in law and politics, to justify that which was once thought to be unjust. Try to think of examples where the use of language in statutes or case law has perverted the original design a legal policy.

BODY HEAT (R; 1981)

Key Themes   Honesty, ethics, legal malpractice
Best Classroom Use: Wills and Trusts, Property

113 minutes   (nudity, sexual situations, profanity, violence)
Cast: William Hurt, Kathleen Turner, Ted Danson, Richard Crenna, J.A. Preston, Mickey Rourke

At the risk of seeming like a prude, *Body Heat* is not recommended for classroom viewing. This film more than earned its R rating, and is more film noir than legal movie. But the key scene described below is definitely worth showing, and is easily understandable with a little background explanation.

Body Heat tells the type of infidelity murder mystery more popular during the 1930s and 1940s, but here without any of that time period's innuendo. When Ned Racine (William Hurt), a small-minded lawyer in a steamy Florida coastal town, comes across the obviously married Mattie Walker (Kathleen Turner), she says something to him in their flirtation that portends Ned's ruination: "You're not too smart; I like that in a man." Drawn in by her sexual power over him, Ned foolishly comes to think that she loves him, his infatuation blocking him from realizing that it was her idea, not his, to murder Mattie's older, rich husband (Richard Crenna). Why a woman with that much voltage would be interested in a 40-watt man never occurs to Ned, a lawyer whose only professional notoriety is the malpractice he committed a few years earlier in drafting a will. So, like a moth to the flame, he thinks he is devising the perfect murder of Mattie's husband, even advising against fraudulently drafting a second will—one that would make Mattie the sole beneficiary of the husband's estate—telling her that such an oddly timed replacement will would look too suspicious.

Nothing goes as planned, or at least as Ned planned, and as Ned's police friends—who are investigating the murder—warn him to stay away from Mattie, the movie heads to its inevitability. Ned hasn't been framed, because he is the murderer, but he can't prove that he didn't act alone, or that Mattie slipped away with the money. What is so enjoyable about this movie is that a few key pieces to the puzzle are sprinkled throughout, helping us and Ned to eventually realize why Mattie was so interested in having an affair with this particular, going nowhere, dim-witted lawyer.

Key Scene—About the only thing Ned did right—amidst the infidelity, murder, and cover-up—was to rebuff Mattie's suggestion that they create a new will for Mattie's husband, since the actual will split the husband's estate between his niece and Mattie, who has been the trophy wife for only a few years. What Ned doesn't realize until this key scene, is that Mattie has gotten into his office and drafted one of her own, forging her husband's and Ned's signatures. When Mattie's dead husband's lawyer gets wind of this new will, he comes to town to meet with all the key parties. What Ned finds out with us is that the new will, although nearly identical to the former will, violates the rule against perpetuities in one of its bequests. According to the Miami lawyer, that flaw makes the new will void, putting the estate into intestacy, resulting in the widow Mattie inheriting everything. Imagine that.

Discussion Suggestion—Discuss the rule against perpetuities, what it is, and how it could be violated. This doctrine from property law is famously inscrutable, and all the more so to legal students. Research your own jurisdiction's law on the rule against perpetuities and whether such a flaw would render a will invalid. Assuming the new will was invalid (as declared by the Miami lawyer), would that result in intestacy or would it revive the prior will? Assuming the niece couldn't inherit half of her rich uncle's estate, could she have successfully sued Ned Racine for malpractice, as an intended third-party beneficiary?

CHANGING LANES (R; 2002)

Key Themes: Fraud and deceit in the practice of law, revenge
Best Classroom Use: Legal Ethics, Estates and Trusts

99 minutes   (strong language)
Cast: Samuel L. Jackson, Ben Affleck, Sydney Pollack, Toni Collette, William Hurt,
               Amanda Peet

Changing Lanes, a powerful and distressing film, is so good at scratching open scabs of past moral failings by so many of its characters that it deserves to be shown to more than just legal students. Two men are driving to court on the FDR expressway on Good Friday. The first driver, Doyle Gipson (Samuel L. Jackson), is a new convert to Alcoholics Anonymous on his way to family court trying to keep his two boys from moving far away with their mother. In furtherance of that goal, Doyle has just purchased a small house where the boys and their mother can live. The other driver is Gavin Banek (Ben Affleck), a recent convert to blind ambition on his way to probate court to close the estate of a philanthropist whose granddaughter is alleging lacked testamentary capacity to remove the board members from his huge foundation shortly before his death, thus giving control over the assets to two senior partners at Banek's firm. In furtherance of his goal, Gavin has important documents, including the philanthropist's power of appointment.

After a minor fender bender on the FDR, Doyle is intent upon following the proper procedures and exchange of insurance information. Gavin simply writes him a blank check and drives away in his Mercedes, offering a "better luck next time" cliché. But in the rush of the moment, Gavin has left his red folder—the one with the power of appointment—with Doyle. When Gavin gets to the courtroom and realizes the key legal documents transferring control over a $100 million foundation are missing, he gets a day-long reprieve from the judge to get the file back. When Doyle gets to his courtroom twenty minutes late, custody has just been granted to his ex-wife in his absence.

Driving through the rain, Gavin spots Doyle walking down the street. After Doyle refuses to give back Gavin's file, exclaiming, "Can you give me my 20 minutes back?" the two men set about to destroy each other, Back at the firm—run by his father-in-law—Gavin's former paramour (Toni Collette) has an idea to get the file back. She knows a hacker who can ruin Doyle's financial history with a few key strokes on a computer, but which can be restored as easily once the file is returned. Doyle gets the threat, but things don't go as anyone planned.

Something else is awry. It finally dawns on Gavin that there was no reason why he should have been in probate court that morning trying push a power of appointment and other trust documents down the throat of a disgruntled granddaughter. One of the two lawyers who are the named trustees should have been in his place. Realizing that he was denied access to the file, and was only given the signature document, Gavin suspects that those two lawyers—his father-in-law and another senior partner—defrauded an infirm man near death and wrote themselves a $1.5 million fee for doing so.

As the movie intersperses between Gavin and Doyle's ever-escalating revenge tactics, there are poignant moments of contemplation and redemptive action. Gavin's father-in-law, however, is not feeling so redemptive, and his solution to the problem of the missing power of appointment is priceless in its brazenness. *Changing Lanes* is worthy of multiple viewings because, like a prism, there are multiple images to notice, all in need of reflection.

Key Scene—As Gavin gets to court, only to realize that the key document, the power of appointment, is missing from his attaché, he tells the judge that the other guy from the accident has it and that it's just a phone call away, which is a lie. The judge gives him until the end of the day to get the original document to court.

Discussion Suggestion—This scene could lead to an analysis of whether original documents are absolutely required in such a situation, or whether a copy from the firm's files would be allowed as a legitimate substitute.

Key Scene—Gavin's epiphany about being used by his father-in-law to extract a signature from a dying man leads him straight to his father-in-law's office. Gavin's father-in-law's reaction to Gavin's plight is brutal, while the other partner's reaction is expeditiously and appallingly fraudulent: reformat the power of appointment to the same length as the living will in the file, and then transfer that signature page to the new power of appointment. Soon after, Gavin sees that the file shows the $1.5 million payment to the two lawyers.

Discussion Suggestion—Aside from acknowledging the legal ethics equivalent of homicide being committed by the elder lawyers, discuss what Gavin, working for his father-in-law, could do about the situation he has unwittingly walked into? Is it too easy to say that Gavin should report the fraud to the court? If he did, what would be his own consequences?

Key Scene—Gavin (with a confessional letter to the probate judge in hand) and his father-in-law have quite a discussion about honesty and cheating. The father-in-law (played by the famous director Sidney Pollack) delivers a short dissertation on situational ethics so poisonously appealing, it almost makes sense. He begins by asking Gavin to contemplate how their dead client amassed such a fortune that he could fund a huge, charitable foundation. Then he delivers the ultimate rationalization made by those who have long since deluded themselves and lost their way: "At the end of the day, I think I do more good than harm. What other standard have I got to judge by?"

Discussion Suggestion—Consider whether Gavin's father-in-law is actually making sense. Isn't situational ethics acceptable in many circles? And if you watch the entire film, discuss Gavin's eventual decision about the trust document fraud. Is his solution any better, or no different, than his father-in-law's?

A CIVIL ACTION (PG-13; 1998)

Key Themes: Litigation strategies and injustice, discovery tactics, hardball negotiation
Best Classroom Use: Civil Procedure, Litigation, Torts, Alternative Dispute Resolution,
                              Legal Ethics

115 minutes   (strong language)
Cast: John Travolta, Robert Duvall, Kathleen Quinlan, Tony Shalhoub,
            William H. Macy, John Lithgow, James Gandolfini

This thoroughly sad movie is a well-crafted story about a litigation nightmare and is perfect for classroom viewing. This is not a John Grisham story in more ways than one, starting with the fact that it's based on a true story, an even sadder book with the same name. In fact, there is a documentary companion to the book, presented chronologically from the beginning of the litigation through pretrial motions, trial, and post-trial motions, which includes official documents from the actual case. At almost 800 pages and designed for law school students, the companion may be more than is necessary for college students, but it would make a great supplement to a civil procedure or litigation class. Except for *The Rainmaker*, perhaps, no other legal movie has so many scenes that are goldmines for class discussion, ranging from litigation to legal ethics to negotiation.

Hotshot attorney Jan Schlictmann (John Travolta) drives a black Porsche and is on Boston's top 10 bachelors list. He has gotten rich and famous by smartly choosing the right kind of personal injury cases for his small firm and often settling them. Against his better judgment, he agrees to take the collective cases of some Woburn, Massachusetts, families who believe their children have suffered disease and death due to poisons in their drinking water as a result of toxic waste dumping. Jan knows better, that this case is an orphan for a reason, but takes it after meeting with the families, focusing his sights on two large, industrial companies, Beatrice Foods, and W.R. Grace. Jan makes two critical decisions upon which the movie hinges. First, he and his firm front the litigation costs; and second, he refuses a couple of settlement opportunities because he wants to take the case all the way to trial. The families want to tell the jury and the world their story, and Jan wants them on the stand because he knows what compelling witnesses they will make.

As the case twists and turns through the discovery process, Jan's small firm is bled white working on its only case, paying for experts and geological studies. Beatrice Fodds's attorney Jerome Facher (Robert Duval) realizes Jan's dilemma and uses it to his advantage, while devising a strategy to keep the plaintiffs from ever setting foot in the jury box. The trial judge (John Lithgow) seems to be less than impartial, almost as if he were a third defense team. Like Don Quixote, Jan loses his perspective and, eventually, his firm. The case he never wanted becomes the one he can't give up. All the while there are the poor families waiting and waiting for their view of justice—an apology and a cleaned-up environment.

Key Scene—The film's prologue shows Jan Schlictmann pushing a severely disabled young man in a wheelchair through a courthouse hallway, on their way to the start of the young man's personal injury trial. Jan's voice can be heard off camera as he coldly tells the audience what characteristics make for a great personal injury plaintiff. He says that an injured plaintiff is generally better than a dead one, unless the death was agonizing and slow, that men are more valuable than women, that the perfect plaintiff is a white, male professional cut down in the prime of life, and that a dead child is worth the least of all. Then, right as the trial is to begin, Jan accepts a $2 million settlement offer, written on a sticky note, after having originally refused $1 million. Jan's firm then celebrates its windfall.

Discussion Suggestion—Discuss different types of damages, and why Jan would say what he did about preferring certain plaintiffs over others. Why is a dead plaintiff generally worth less than an injured one? You could use Westlaw® or Lexis® to research what the average verdicts are in your jurisdiction for particular injuries. Discuss why it was that the defense lawyer increased his offer by 100 percent when he did.

Key Scene—Jerome Facher, Beatrice's lead attorney, deposes the plaintiffs, and in a quick montage, asks them a variety of questions about their personal habits, such as whether they or their kids eat peanut butter or bacon, whether they use nonstick pans, whether they have silver fillings in their teeth, and whether they use tampons. One plaintiff, being deposed about his little boy's death, tells the horrible story of how his son died in the car on the way to a medical clinic. After watching the man leave his conference room, Facher says, "These people can never testify."

Discussion Suggestion—Why was Facher so interested in such trifling details about the plaintiffs' habits and lifestyle? How does this relate to defending his client? Sometimes it seems that there is a focus in litigation classes only on the plaintiff's efforts and strategies, and this scene shows a smart defense lawyer at work.

Key Scene—Facher visits Jan at the tannery property where Jan's geological team is digging up the ground, and tells Jan that nothing yet has shown how Facher's client is involved in dumping toxic wastes. But, Facher says, Beatrice is willing to get out of the case by paying for Jan's expenses in the case thus far. That offer is rejected outright, even though immediately before that scene Jan's voice can be heard telling how corrupt trials are and how settlement is the best and smartest way to handle a lawsuit. Then, after some of W.R. Grace's employees are caught lying in their depositions, Grace calls a settlement meeting. During that meeting, Jan makes a demand that goes higher and higher until it reaches $320 million, which is rejected outright.

Discussion Suggestion—Why did Facher offer to settle the case if, as he claimed, Beatrice had no liability? Why did Jan make such a ridiculous offer he knew would never be accepted? That scene shows how maybe Jan had begun to lose his objectivity.

Key Scene—The trial judge agrees with Facher's belief that unless the jury were to find that the defendants actually dumped the chemicals in the water table during the time periods in question, there would be no need for the plaintiffs to testify. Jan is shocked at the judge's decision to bifurcate the trial.

Discussion Suggestion—Realizing Facher's brilliant strategy, discuss what bifurcation is and why the judge thought such a decision was necessary. Could Jan have filed an interlocutory appeal to the judge's decision?

Key Scene—Two fascinating negotiating scenes occur late in the film. The first involves Facher approaching Jan in the courthouse hallway while waiting for the jury to decide the set of technical verdict questions devised by the judge. Facher appeals to Jan's impoverished state, and uses uncertainty as leverage, and then offers Jan $20 million. Jan rejects the offer, only to hear the jury find in favor of Beatrice Foods. Then, W.R. Grace calls Jan to New York City to discuss settling the case, and Jan and his associates discuss what they need to get out of the case—$8 million. In a beautifully shot sequence of flashbacks mixed with present action, Jan and the W.R. Grace executive negotiate. Jan rejects the $8 million offer, and is browbeaten for it by his accountant. Finally overcome, Jan calls W.R. Grace to accept the offer.

Discussion Suggestion—You could have a field day discussing how Jan's team prepared for the negotiation, how they wanted to appear as if they didn't need money, how leverage was used in these connected scenes, and what kind of hardball negotiation tactics were used. Also, students might notice that, as shown, Jan never got his clients' authority to reject or accept any offer.

Key Scene—Jan and his team meet with their clients to explain how the settlement money is to be apportioned. Jan has reduced the fee to 28 percent, which is $2.2 million, and the expenses were $3.5 million. That leaves $375,000 for each family. Sadly, that isn't enough because that isn't what they were ever seeking.

Discussion Suggestion—Discuss the significance of knowing the difference between legal fees and costs, and how a fees agreement should explain whether a contingent fee is to be off the gross or net recovery.

CLASS ACTION (R; 1991)

Key Themes: Litigation and legal ethics, product liability, law firm politics, father/daughter lawyer relationship
Best Classroom Use: Introduction to Paralegal Studies, Litigation, Torts, Legal Ethics

110 minutes   (strong language)
Cast: Gene Hackman, Mary Elizabeth Mastrantonio, Colin Friels, Laurence Fishburne, Joanna Merlin, Fred Thompson

Although *Class Action* could be thought of as another David versus Goliath personal injury story, this overlooked movie is appealing on many levels. It is about a product liability case obviously reminiscent of the Ford Pinto explosion cases of a few decades ago. It is about the tricks used in discovery to bury the other side in paper and red herrings. It is about ethical quandaries high-powered lawyers face. It is also about the tense relationship between a father and daughter, opposite in so many ways, but who are both lawyers and fighting each other in and out of court.

Gene Hackman plays Jedediah Tucker Ward, famous civil rights lawyer and publicity hound, who has taken up a class action lawsuit that had languished with another firm. The plaintiffs are suing Argo Motors for the injuries and deaths suffered as a result of driving in Argo Meridians, which blew up on rear impact. Argo is represented by an august firm, whose rising associate is Maggie Ward (Mary Elizabeth Mastrantonio), Jedediah's daughter. She begs her boss (and boyfriend) to be on the Argo case, not flinching upon learning she'll be opposing her father—something the two have done for years, with Mrs. Ward trying to be the peacemaker.

Jedediah's legal team thinks its case is weak despite the plaintiffs' horrible injuries, because nothing in discovery has led to a design defect in the Meridian that would have caused the explosions. But as Maggie is preparing for trial and interviewing key Argo employees, she discovers that not only was there a defect in the turn signals' electronics, but Argo was aware of it from the beginning and had hidden that from her and the plaintiffs. Despite what Argo's chief researcher told them in writing when the Meridian was being built, Argo's executives believed it cheaper to deal with the lawsuits when some of the cars would blow up, instead of recalling the Meridian. To make matters worse, Argo's plausible deniability was based on earlier advice by its lawyer, Maggie's boss and boyfriend, who is now trying to cover his gross malpractice by forcing Maggie to be a team player.

Believing she was hoodwinked, Maggie visits the firm's senior partner and namesake, only to find that his solution is to promise Maggie a partnership for covering up the truth. Knowing that her client is about to get away with its deadly fraud, and that, thanks to the deceitfulness of her partners, her father will never be able to find the evidence he would have otherwise found, Maggie is faced with quite a dilemma. Her solution leaves the viewer cheering, but one might wonder if fighting fire with fire would actually get Maggie burned for violating her duty of loyalty to the client.

Key Scene—Maggie begs her boss to be put on the Argo defense team, criticizing the competence of a colleague who is also interested in working on the Argo case, and who has recommended settling. Maggie's boss agrees to put her on the team, alerting her that her father is now representing the plaintiffs. As the viewer comes to learn, Maggie and her boss are dating each other, compounding the problems Maggie will face.

Discussion Suggestion—Although fictionalized in many legal films and television shows, law office romances are all too often nonfiction, and risky. Should the rule generally prohibiting lawyers and clients from dating each other also apply to in-office romances?

Key Scene—Father and daughter face off in court for the first time in a discovery motion hearing. He is asking the court to order Argo to turn over the names, job descriptions, and current addresses of all Argo employees who worked on the Meridian from 1980—1985. She claims that is too onerous a request for her client. He tells the judge how easy it was for him—making a phony phone call to Argo—to get the current address of a particular Argo retiree, belying her claim that Argo can't be expected to comply with such a time-consuming demand. The judge sides with him. Tragically, a few minutes later, Mrs. Ward dies of a heart attack in the courthouse hallway.

Discussion Suggestion—Discuss the nature of the discovery process, and whether a defendant such as Argo is likely to ever win such a motion. What would Jedediah want with all those names and related information? Did he violate any ethics rule in what he did to get the address of an Argo retiree, such as the rule on dealing with unrepresented persons?

Key Scene—In quite a lengthy, but worthwhile group of scenes, Maggie comes to realize that Argo Motors has been hiding the truth about its defective Meridian, and that the key principals at her firm, including her boyfriend and direct supervisor, are active in the cover-up. After finding the researcher whose tests warned Argo that the Meridian was dangerous, Maggie makes a copy of the incriminating memorandum and dresses down Argo's chief of engineering, who had earlier told her that the Meridian was always shown to be safe. His calm defense to her charges is that he relied on the advice of Argo's lawyer back then, who is Maggie's boyfriend now. Maggie then realizes what her boyfriend was doing by putting her on the Argo team, betting that she would cover for his prior malpractice because of their relationship. So, off to the senior partner she goes. His solution is to bury the safety memorandum amid boxes and boxes of discovery materials, claiming that is within the letter of the law. He suggests that a mistake in the discovery materials log would even make it harder for Jedediah to find what they've "given" him. But Maggie's boyfriend has a better idea: Remove the listing all together from the discovery log and take a copy of the Meridian safety memorandum from Maggie's locked desk. After seeing the senior partner a second time, Maggie is promised a partnership to keep her mouth shut.

Discussion Suggestion—There is much to chew on here. Discuss how the duty of confidentiality bears on Maggie's knowledge of Argo's cover-up. Analyze the strategy of burying key documentary evidence among other discovery materials, like a needle in a haystack. Is it wrong or crafty, or both? Does Maggie have a duty to report to the trial judge what she knows about her bosses' behavior?

Key Scene—Having set her trap, Maggie is able to sit back and watch in court as her father calls Maggie's boss to the stand and gets him to lie under oath about having never seen the missing safety memorandum. Then, an accountant at Argo is called to the stand and testifies that he had discussions about that memorandum, and the company's decision not to recall the Meridian. Maggie's senior partner is flabbergasted, and accuses her of giving privileged documents to her father. His protests fall on deaf ears, and soon he is trying to settle the case to save his own hide.

Discussion Suggestion—Has Maggie violated the duty of confidentiality and loyalty to her client by assisting the plaintiff in locating, through triangulation, the key evidence it is seeking? If she is aware of a fraud being committed on the court, can she unilaterally disclose the fraud to the opposing party, at least without informing the trial judge?

THE CLIENT (PG-13; 1994)

Key Themes: Honesty in litigation, attorney-client confidentiality
Best Classroom Use: Criminal Procedure, Legal Ethics, Introduction to Paralegal Studies

121 minutes   (violence, strong language)
Cast: Susan Sarandon, Brad Renfro, Tommy Lee Jones, Mary-Louise Parker, Anthony
            LaPaglia, Anthony Edwards

What starts out as an exploration in the woods for two poor young brothers, ends up making one of them catatonic and the other a target for the New Orleans mob. Watching a man commit suicide is awful enough, but for older brother Mark Swayne (Brad Renfro), it is even worse, since he was in the car with the man just before the end. As it turns out, the man was the lawyer for the notorious hit man "The Blade," (Anthony LaPaglia) who was about to go on trial for the murder of a Louisiana senator, even though there is no body. And because that lawyer knew where the body is buried, and had been threatened with a subpoena by the famed federal prosecutor "Reverend Roy" (Tommy Lee Jones), the mob lawyer figured it was better to die at his own hands before The Blade got a hold of him. Since the investigation shows that Mark was in the car with the terrified lawyer before his death, the police and The Blade believe the boy knows the lawyer's secret. Realizing that Mark and his brother are poor and only have a mother, Reverend Roy and his team come north to Memphis, believing it shouldn't be that hard to get Mark to testify about what the lawyer told him. The mob also comes north, believing it shouldn't be that hard to make Mark disappear.

Rightfully believing he needs his own lawyer, Mark ends up in the dingy downtown office of Reggie Love (Susan Sarandon), who Mark at first mistakes for a secretary. Reggie takes his case for the fee of $1. Then begins a cat and mouse—and another cat—game, as Reggie tries to protect her client from two nemeses: Reverend Roy, who tries to cajole and threaten Mark into testifying for the government; and The Blade, who is doing everything possible to prevent Mark from having any say in the matter.

Because this movie comes from a John Grisham book, there is little doubt that Memphis Mark will survive both the duplicitously carnivorous Reverend Roy and the just plain carnivorous mobsters, and that Reggie Love will use barely legal tactics to navigate through shark-infested waters. What might go unnoticed in the film is that the lawyer's suicide is prompted by the threat of a subpoena to testify against his client concerning the whereabouts of the missing senator's body. This is a curious setup for a movie about attorney-client confidentiality, since a client's prior crimes are covered by the ethics rules on confidentiality, as well as evidentiary statutes on attorney-client privilege. Although not expressly stated, Anthony Edward's character seems like Susan Sarandon's character's paralegal, which is a welcome role reversal.

Key Scene—While waiting in the hospital for his little brother, Mark witnesses an ambulance chaser solicit a patient in a wheelchair, leaving an advertising flyer. Mark takes the flyer and heads to the city office building looking for that lawyer, and through happenstance walks into Reggie Love's office. Soon thereafter, Mark questions her about becoming his lawyer, including asking her about the meaning of confidentiality. Eventually, she takes his case for $1.

Discussion Suggestion—Analyze the ambulance chaser's actions in light of your jurisdiction's solicitation rules, and examine whether Reggie's statements to Mark about lawyer confidentiality are accurate.

Key Scene—The first time Mark Swayne meets with Reverend Roy and his team of prosecutors and FBI agents, they are unaware that he has retained the services of Reggie Love, and proceed to lie in response to his questions about whether he needs his mother with him and if he should have a lawyer. What Reverend Roy doesn't know is that Mark is secretly tape recording the meeting and, upon leaving for the bathroom he returns with Reggie, where she proceeds to dress down the Reverend and show him the tape.

Discussion Suggestion—Discuss Reverend Roy's actions, particularly telling a child that he must testify or else could be charged with obstruction of justice, and whether it violates any rules of ethics, or worse. If there is time, research your jurisdiction's law and see if Reverend Roy or Reggie Love could get in trouble for what they did.

CRIMINAL LAW (R; 1989)

Key Themes: Miscarriage of justice, attorney-client confidentiality, vigilantism
Best Classroom Use: Criminal Law, Legal Ethics, Interviewing

112 minutes   (violence, sexual situation, strong language)
Cast: Gary Oldman, Kevin Bacon, Karen Young, Tess Harper

When a movie about a criminal defense lawyer opens with a Nietzsche quote ("Whoever fights monsters should see to it that in the process he does not become a monster."), you know you are in for something extreme. *Criminal Law*, a B-movie about a defense attorney turned vigilante, is neither high art nor realistic, but there are a few scenes worth showing and discussing.

Ben Chase (Gary Oldman), formally of the prosecutor's office, is an up and coming criminal defense attorney in Boston, and is defending Martin Thiel IV (Kevin Bacon), a rich preppie accused of the grisly rape and murder of a young woman. The key evidence against Martin is eyewitness testimony, and Ben succeeds in providing reasonable doubt through his cross-examination of the key witness and by using a sneaky trial tactic. After securing his smug client's freedom, Ben's peacock-like strut is cut short when, a few nights later, another grisly rape and murder are committed and Ben is left with the inescapable conclusion that the murderer is his client, who summoned Ben to a late night meeting in the park so that Ben could find the victim. Wracked with guilt, Ben contacts a sex crimes detective and former colleague, and tells her of his plan for atonement: He is going to represent Martin again and gather evidence against his client. Obviously, such a strategy is not only ludicrous and career ending, but it is miscast, since Ben bears no personal responsibility for the second and third murders.

Every defense lawyer faces the possibility that his or her client might not be as innocent as their plea indicates. Since Ben actually believes in his client at the movie's beginning, Ben's regret for his "role" in the murders belies his persona as a tough defense lawyer. What then follows is a thriller that somehow manages to weave an abortion plot line into its explanation of the murderer's psychotic motivation.

Key Scene—Early in the film, Ben is defending Martin against the original rape and murder charge by telling the jury in his opening statement that the case is based on eyewitness testimony, which will be proven mistaken. Ben then cross-examines the state's key witness, who claims to have seen Martin near the body. She was on her way to get some diapers for her baby when she saw Martin in the street during a rain storm, and Ben's cross-examination, while inappropriately harsh against a woman with no axe to grind, shows how doubts can be raised about one's belief in what they saw. Then, Ben calls his last witness, someone wrongly imprisoned for murder because of eyewitness mistakes, and who displays a poster of his face next to the real murderer's face (over the objection of the prosecution).

Discussion Suggestion—Provided you have given the class a little background explanation about what preceded the cross-examination and direct-examination scenes, discuss the peculiarity of Ben's diapers question. It is an interesting example of a probe question (searching for what is behind an initial answer, to see if there is something worthwhile), which paralegals should be able to skillfully raise in client and witness interview settings. Also discuss whether the wrongly imprisoned witness's testimony could ever be allowed in under the evidence rules. Finally, discuss the pros and cons of eyewitness testimony, and how recent research shows it to be highly fallible.

Key Scene—After being confronted in his office by the best friend of the murder victim Ben found in the park, Ben stops her from leaving through the use of some unsettling physical force and then proceeds to tell her his plan on catching his client and bringing him to justice. Through that scene and the next, where he asks for the help of the sex crimes detective in catching his client red handed, Ben discloses client confidences and sets his client up to be caught.

Discussion Suggestion—Obviously, there is nothing realistic about this scene. However, you could discuss two topics after watching it. First, determine how many professional responsibility rules Ben violated in those five minutes. Second, analyze what, if anything, Ben could lawfully do if he believes his client has gotten away with murder and committed another one.

DISCLOSURE (R; 1994)

Key Themes: Sexual harassment, mediation
Best Classroom Use: Employment Law, Alternative Dispute Resolution

129 minutes   (sexual situation, explicit sexual discussions, strong language)
Cast: Michael Douglas, Demi Moore, Donald Sutherland, Caroline Goodall, Roma
               Maffia, Dennis Miller

Of the possible ways in which sexual harassment can occur, that which is most often thought of is when an employer conditions hiring, promoting, or firing decisions on the employee's submission to sexual conduct. Traditionally, such unlawful behavior has often been associated with male supervisors. *Disclosure*, based on Michael Crichton's best seller, takes the stereotype and twists it by making the supervisor a woman, and the subordinate a man. Although this film unrealistically takes place over a five-day work week, it provides plenty of material that would be fitting for an employment law, or alternative dispute resolution class. However, due to the explicit sexual nature of this film, only certain scenes might be fitting for a classroom, lest the instructor be accused of harassment by showing all of *Disclosure*.

Tom Sanders (Michael Douglas) is an executive at DigiCom, a Seattle software company, and is in charge of bringing to market a new virtual reality CD-ROM data storage device, which is a key factor in a merger DigiCom is near concluding. As we meet Tom heading to work on Monday, he is about to learn if he has been chosen as vice president at his company. When he gets to the office, he learns that not only was he passed over, but that the position was given to Meredith Johnson (Demi Moore), an old flame of his from his single days. By the time she calls him up to her office for a late night meeting, Tom's buddies think something is going on, especially since they know of his wandering eyes and shoulder rubbing ways. What happens in her office that night seems to be clear: She makes explicit advances towards him, he succumbs but then stops before they have intercourse, and she threatens him as he leaves her office.

The next day, Tom finds out that Meredith has accused him of sexual harassment, and DigiCom wants Tom to quietly acknowledge his wrongdoing by moving to the company's Austin, Texas division. Stunned and furious, Tom hires a notorious civil rights attorney and accuses Meredith of sexual harassment, hoping that the threat of a suit and its attendant publicity will force DigiCom to settle with him before Friday's scheduled merger announcement, and before his wife finds out about the whole mess. What follows is a look at the dirtiest of corporate backstabbing, an unrealistic glance at mediation, an examination of the sexual politics of men and women in the workplace, and a desperate hunt for who is behind the sabotage of the virtual reality device that is critical to the DigiCom merger.

The Bureau of National Affairs provides a very interesting sample of a confidential statement for a mediation, which is based exactly on the fact pattern in *Disclosure*. Using the same parties and facts, this plaintiff's confidential statement would be a nice supplement in an ADR course, or in a litigation course discussing mediation. The sample, a PDF file, can be accessed at: bna.com/bnabooks/ababna/rnr/2004/err284.pdf.

Key Scene—Not realizing that Meredith has beaten him to the punch, Tom is approached by Philip Blackburn, DigiCom's human resources director, who is quite the Brutus. Telling Meredith's version of the preceding night's events, Blackburn almost consolingly encourages Tom to simply acknowledge his harassing activities by leaving Seattle and moving to a DigiCom location in Austin, Texas. Tom protests his innocence, and claims that it was Meredith who made the advances at him and that she was the harasser.

Discussion Suggestion—In an employment law class, analyze this scene in light of appropriate employment law and human resource policy. If one employee has made a claim of sexual harassment against another, what would be the legally appropriate response by the human resources office? Also, discuss whether Meredith (the boss) could legally be sexually harassed by Tom (the subordinate). If so, under what circumstances?

Key Scene—[There are actually a collection of related scenes involving a mediation, but the first extended scene would be sufficient.] By Wednesday, two days after the Monday night imbroglio, somehow a mediation occurs between Tom, Meredith and DigiCom, with a judge serving as the mediator. Unfortunately, the mediation scenes, which are pivotal to the final act in *Disclosure*, are unrealistic. Instead of seeing a mediator attempt to identify interests with the parties and seek options for a possible solution acceptable to both sides, what we get looks more like depositions, with a court reporter taking down the direct and cross-examinations of Tom, Meredith, and other witnesses. In fact, the judge/mediator only serves as a referee between the lawyers and their tactics. The eventual settlement offer DigiCom makes to Tom is a result of key evidence Tom recovers that conclusively establishes his version of events.

Discussion Suggestion—Using the sample confidential statement discussed above, analyze the mediation scene for what it could have been, had it really been a mediation. From what has been presented in the film up to that point, is there anything that can be mediated? If so, what interests might be uncovered in mediation?

Erin Brockovich (R; 2000)

Key Themes: Toxic waste litigation, paralegal efforts, corporate fraud, overcoming personal and legal odds

Best Classroom Use: Introduction to Paralegal Studies, Litigation, Torts, Legal Ethics

131 minutes   (strong language, provocative scenes)
Cast: Julia Roberts, Albert Finney, Aaron Eckhart, Marg Helgenberger

Erin Brockovich might be the film on this list that is capable of generating the most energetic class discussion, and not simply because its title character is the country's most famous—and beloved—paralegal. Julia Roberts won a Best Actress Oscar for capturing the desperation and ingenuity of Erin Brockovich, a woman who fights demographic prejudice to keep an otherwise unwinnable case against a powerful corporation alive. Like a hero from Greek tragedy, Ms. Brockovich's flaws make her more than one-dimensional. Those interested in pursuing beyond the film's version of events might start with an April 14, 2000, Salon.com article that claims only the positive half of the *Erin Brockovich* story was presented, and that some of the actual plaintiffs have less than charitable feelings towards their legal team.

Erin Brockovich is a struggling, single mother of three, searching for work and a babysitter. After getting t-boned at a red light and suing the doctor who hit her, Erin loses at trial, in no small measure due to her foul-mouthed performance on the witness stand. Somehow, she talks her way into a job with Ed Masry (Albert Finney), her lawyer from the car accident suit. Having a never-take-no-for-an-answer attitude trumps having no education or legal experience, and it is that attitude that leads her to the biggest tort case of its time. While going through a *pro bono* real estate file, Erin notices medical records for persons in Hinkley, California, whose homes are being purchased by Pacific Gas & Electric (PG&E), a utility company operating a facility nearby. Using charm and her feminine wiles in her investigation (to put it mildly), Erin comes to believe that PG&E's use of chromium 6 has polluted the water, resulting in cancers and other illness for many of Hinkley's residents.

After Ed fires and rehires Erin, they begin their representation of the Hinkley residents, all of whom are so significant to Erin she has memorized their personal information and history. Initially, Ed's strategy is to avoid a lawsuit against PG&E (for fear of it being dismissed out of hand) and, instead, to negotiate better real estate settlements. Finally convinced by Erin's persistence, Ed files suit against PG&E. As the burdens of the case mount against Ed and his small firm Erin tries to balance motherhood, work, and a relationship with a gentle and long-suffering neighbor.

Against Erin's strident and scathing wishes, Ed links up with a high-powered litigator from Los Angeles, believing this will provide the financing and expertise the case needs. The new lawyer's tactic is binding arbitration, rather than a lengthy trial. This change of plans has the plaintiffs so upset, many of them are planning on jumping ship. So once again, Erin comes to the rescue, succeeding in securing consent to arbitrate from enough of the plaintiffs, as well as finding the case's missing key link—internal documents tying the corruption of the Hinkley PG&E to its corporate parent. Erin's efforts are so fruitful, the plaintiffs are awarded $333 million, and Erin is awarded a $2 million bonus. *Erin Brockovich* is definitely not *A Civil Action*.

Key Scene—Early in her time at Masry's firm, Erin is given the real estate file that leads to the PG&E case. Concerned by Erin's low blouses and short skirts, Ed tells her to consider dressing differently. In no uncertain terms, Erin tells Ed she'll dress the way she wants to. Erin's provocative style of dressing, and her use of cleavage, is integral to the plotline. Later, after Ed rehires Erin—realizing she wasn't AWOL, but was investigating the Hinkley cases and researching chromium 6 records at the water board office—he asks her what makes her think that she could go back to the water board and convince its employee to allow her to search for more, critical records. Her answer: "They're called boobs, Ed."

Discussion Suggestion—Has Erin succeeded because of her appearance? Is it shrewd or lewd to use one's physical attributes to get what is needed in a professional environment? Presently, would there be any alternate methods a paralegal could use to search for the same information Erin is seeking at the water board? Working paralegals might want to discuss the efficacy of talking to one's boss the way Erin does throughout the film.

Key Scene—Ed and Erin meet with some of the Hinkley families who are prospective clients, and Ed encourages them to sign with his firm. He explains that PG&E vaguely told them about the water problem possibility in order to get the one-year statute of limitations started, thereby preventing the families from eventually filing claims. Ed tells the families that his fee is 40 percent of whatever the plaintiffs receive and Erin, in order to combat the families' reticence, tells them they will owe Ed nothing, including costs, if they lose. They agree to the representation, and Erin begins going door-to-door attempting to find more plaintiffs.

Discussion Suggestion—Discuss the statute of limitations conundrum presented in this scene, as well as Erin's fees explanation—the rare statement that even the case's costs will be borne by the lawyer, no matter what. Also, Erin's solicitation might be a good topic for conversation. Does it comport with the generally strict solicitation rules? Would it matter if the case was a class action?

Key Scene—At the film's conclusion, Ed and his team have moved into a much loftier office space, and the new furniture is being delivered. Ed enters Erin's office and hands her a bonus check of $2 million.

Discussion Suggestion—Does this bonus violate the rule against fee sharing with a paralegal? Research your jurisdiction's fee sharing rule to see whether this type of payment would be allowed. Should there be any prohibitions on whether a lawyer can share part of his or her fee with a paralegal?

A FEW GOOD MEN (R; 1992)

Key Themes: Military justice, the defense of superior orders, courtroom strategies
Best Classroom Use: Criminal Law, Introduction to Paralegal Studies

138 minutes   (strong language)
Cast: Tom Cruise, Demi Moore, Jack Nicholson, Kevin Bacon, Kiefer Sutherland

Certain lines from movie history are so memorable as to almost become trite: "We'll always have Paris," "I see dead people," "Show me the money," and "You can't handle the truth!" Yet, Jack Nicholson's notorious witness stand snarl still resonates, particularly in post-9/11 America, where the debate over the military's methods—particularly at Guantanomo Bay—of protecting us never seems to wane. From a play by Aaron Sorkin, the writer of "The West Wing," *A Few Good Men* is a well-made courtroom drama that deals with the defense of superior orders in a unique way. Here, it is used as a defense to a murder committed against a comrade, not the enemy.

After two marines are charged with murdering Private William Santiago at Guantanomo Bay, Cuba, Navy JAG lawyer Daniel Kaffee (Tom Cruise) is assigned to defend them, over the wishes of Lt. Commander JoAnne Galloway (Demi Moore), who believes the killing is a result of a hazing procedure—a Code Red—gone awry. Private Santiago was a disgruntled grunt who had been writing letters to politicians begging to be transferred from Guantanomo in exchange for revealing the facts of a marine's wrongful discharge of a rifle into communist Cuba. The base commander, Col. Nathan Jessup (Jack Nicholson), is an old school marine who is thought to be next in line for a prominent position at the National Security Agency. JoAnne thinks the accused marines are being hung out to dry for the good of the Corps, and Kaffees' appointment as their chief defender adds to her suspicion, since Kaffee is barely out of law school, and is known for plea bargaining everything. To the arrogant Kaffee with the famous legal pedigree, nothing is more important than a softball game, and JoAnne strains to convince him that these two mum marines need to defend themselves by violating their code of loyalty and telling what they know about the secret—and illegal—practice of a Code Red.

Assuming that Kaffee and JoAnne could prove that a Code Red had been ordered, then ultimate responsibility would lie with Col. Jessup, whose smile is even intimidating. Not only does Jessup deny giving an order for a Code Red, he claims he ordered that the weak Santiago not be touched. Furthermore, the records show that Jessup had approved Santiago's transfer request, which was to take effect hours before Santiago was killed. All of Jessup's staff seems to be in lock step with that story, leaving Kaffee and JoAnne to prepare for a murder trial with two defendants who are not telling the whole story. These lawyers have no defense—other than to claim that their clients were following unwritten orders to violently punish a lazy and troublemaking fellow soldier, which, if provable, would still be an illegal act. The courtroom fireworks occurring during the climactic showdown between Kaffee and Jessup are provocative, and the ending is bittersweet.

Key Scene—Early in the film, a JAG prosecutor approaches Kaffee on the softball diamond to discuss a case in which they're involved. A sailor has been charged with possession of marijuana and Kaffee, representing the sailor, has done nothing so far. The prosecutor threatens Kaffee with warnings about the sailor's impending court martial and prison sentence. Unfazed, Kaffee reminds the prosecutor that the sailor bought a bag or oregano, thinking it was marijuana, which is not the crime the prosecutor is making it out to be. The prosecutor bristles even more, to which Kaffee threatens to bury the prosecutor in pretrial paperwork and motions if the prosecutor goes forward with those charges. After some wrangling, the prosecutor agrees to plead the case down to a C misdemeanor, with no incarceration.

Discussion Suggestion—Considering that most civil and criminal cases end through settlement or plea bargaining, this scene is illustrative. Discuss what Kaffee had as bargaining chips or leverage, and what made the prosecutor agree to settle a case he seemed so intent on prosecuting. What is gained through plea bargaining?

Key Scene—Kaffee and JoAnne go to Guantanomo to interview Col. Jessup and his staff. Jessup is pleasant with small talk, but exercising dominance over the interviewers. Jessup states that Santiago was going to be transferred from Guantanomo by way of a 6:00 A.M. flight on the morning of his death, and JoAnne asks Jessup pointed questions about the use of Code Reds in the marines. Kaffee tries to stop her line of questioning and Jessup responds to it in a most foul and sexist manner. As Kaffee and JoAnne are getting up to leave, Kaffee pauses to ask Jessup for a copy of Santiago's transfer order. This throws Jessup into a slow burn, and he begins to verbally assault Kaffee about Kaffee's lack of respect for Jessup.

Discussion Suggestion—Presaging the eventual showdown over whether Jessup actually ordered the Code Red for Santiago, this scene is a good one to discuss on how to handle witness interviews. Notice how both Kaffee and JoAnne were prepared for their meeting with Jessup and his staff. Even though JoAnne's questions about Code Reds might have been intended to show her lack of tact, compared to Kaffee's, her questions are strong follow-up questions. Kaffee's request to Jessup for Santiago's transfer order is a fine example of how a probe question can uncover something important. Here, Jessup's vitriolic response to the question was more valuable to Kaffee's understanding of the case than the alleged transfer order.

Key Scene—Kaffee gets Jessup on the witness stand, hoping to get Jessup to admit he ordered the Code Red that led to the young marines being charged with murder. Because Kaffee has no evidence against Jessup, Kaffee is on very thin ice, and his only hope is to goad Jessup and trust that Jessup's old-fashioned machismo will come out. And does it ever. Jessup finally, and with gusto, proudly states he ordered the Code Red, and then makes his famous speech on the necessity of having men like him in the military protecting us from our enemies. His compact speech on his unsavory role as guardian of our freedoms is forceful and compelling. He is like the butcher defending his role when accused by a customer of cruelty to animals. Jessup's testimony leads to his arrest, much to his astonishment, and the jury finds the two marines not guilty of murder or conspiracy. They are, however, convicted of conduct unbecoming a marine, and are dishonorably discharged.

Discussion Suggestion—There is a lot to chew on in this lengthy scene. From a technical standpoint, notice how Kaffee's questioning and demeanor lead to Jessup being trapped in his inconsistent statements. Angered by this realization, and by his own sense of justice, it finally caused him to proudly proclaim what he had been begrudgingly denying. More importantly, there is a huge discussion point here involving Jessup's views and the marines' superior orders defense, which is a variation of the defense of duress. Despite the ugliness of his position, is Jessup right when he says that the death of Santiago saved lives? Don't we need men like Jessup to keep us safe in today's world, as much as we're loathe to admit it? Or is he a relic of an unnecessarily brutal, bygone era? As for the marines on trial, isn't their claim that they were following orders as hollow for them as it would be for any other person accused of a crime? As is mentioned in the film, that defense was used at Nuhremburg and at Mai Lai, both to no avail. Research your jurisdiction's defense of duress to see if there is any room for one to claim he or she was following orders.

THE FIRM (R; 1993)

Key Themes: Corrupt lawyers, blackmail, racketeering, overbilling
Best Classroom Use: Legal Ethics, Criminal Law, Introduction to Paralegal Studies

153 minutes   (strong language, sexual situations, violence)
Cast: Tom Cruise, Jeanne Tripplehorn, Gene Hackman, Ed Harris, Holly Hunter, Hal
               Holbrook, Wilford Brimley

One of the first John Grisham novels to be made into a movie, *The Firm* is an effective legal thriller that put Tom Cruise on the horns of a dilemma—surviving in a corrupt law firm with a high death rate for associates who know too much, or dealing with a Justice Department whose plans for him include turning state's evidence, losing his law license, and entering the witness protection program. Rare is the thriller whose climax is connected to legal bills and attorney-client confidentiality.

Tom Cruise plays eager Harvard law school grad, Mitch McDeere, a guy from the wrong side of the tracks who ranks fifth in his class and who is being courted by big city law firms with much to offer him. But Mitch is seduced by an even richer tender from Bendini, Lambert, & Locke, a small Memphis firm that seems to have family values, which would be wonderful, except that the family they value is the Mafia. The firm seems a little too perfect, with its provision of a house and mortgage, a country club membership, and a Mercedes. But the firm disapproves of Mitch's wife (Jeanne Tripplehorn) working outside the home. It also has a full-time security detail who bugs everything (including Mitch's house), and has lost more than a few associates to untimely accidents. As Mitch is beginning his career and studying for the bar exam, he is approached by an FBI agent (Ed Harris) who soon informs Mitch that this perfect law firm for whom he works is in cahoots with the Mafia. Mitch is told that his only alternative to literally being worked to death is to help the Justice Department gather evidence against the firm, which will be ruinous to Mitch's and his wife's lives, not to mention his law license. And so the idyllic life becomes horrific.

Facing the prospects of being blackmailed by both the firm and the government, and losing his marriage to an indiscretion, Mitch begins to collect the evidence of money laundering his firm has been doing for the mob for years, knowing that some of the files are in a condominium closet in the Grand Cayman Islands. While preparing for his own ruination and negotiating a deal with the government to get his older brother out of prison, Mitch realizes there might be another way out of this mess. A disgruntled client has a meeting with Mitch to complain about how much Mitch had overbilled him, something the client says has been going on for years. Mitch is surprised since he knows he didn't do that when he filled out his time sheet. Even the client knows that the firm is committing mail fraud—a serious felony—every time it mails falsely stated client bills. Now Mitch believes that if he can gather evidence of the illegal billing instead of the money laundering, he can save his life and career, assuming the firm's security thugs don't kill him first. In order to accomplish his plan, Mitch needs the help of one of his clients, the Chicago Mafia boss, provided the mobster understands the significance of attorney-client confidentiality.

Key Scene—Mitch McDeere is scurrying between job interviews with prestigious law firms headquartered in America's largest cities. The interviewers are regaling him with the specifics of their employment offers, including large salaries and prime sporting event tickets. Then, Mitch interviews with the key principals at Bendini, Lambert, & Locke. Here, he lies when questioned about his family background, and they lie about almost everything except the financial inducements, which include a 20 percent premium over the highest offer any other firm made to Mitch. Much is made about the benefits of life in Memphis and the family atmosphere at the firm. Mitch then tells his wife about the offer and, eventually, he takes the bait.

Discussion Suggestion—In an Introduction to Law or Legal Ethics class, you could discuss what type of employment (private practice, corporate, or government) your students are seeking and what they are looking for in a job. What really matters to them? For some, quality of life, benefits, or flexibility matter more than an hourly wage or salary.

Key Scene—Mitch's epiphany occurs when he visits a non-Mafia client, who has a complaint about his bill. It seems the bill reflected 33 hours of Mitch's time, which the client knows was wildly exaggerated. Mitch is surprised by the complaint and tells his client that he turned in a different time sheet to the billing department. The client responds, "This overbilling has gotten so common, nobody gives it another thought," and "when somebody put a stamp on it and mailed it, it became a federal offense." At this point, Mitch realizes there might be a way to bring down the firm without having to lose his livelihood by informing the government about the firm's clients' illegal activities. Instead, he can inform the government about the firm's mail fraud, provided the Mafia clients agree to release their billing records.

Discussion Suggestion—If you have watched the prior scenes in the film, or are aware of its general plot, discuss what Mitch would have to offer the government in the first place. Mitch wasn't a party to any of the crimes the FBI has been investigating, so what threat could the government be holding over him to force him to even consider telling on his firm's clients' illegal activities? Beyond that, wouldn't Mitch be immune from any threat or subpoena since he is bound by both ethics rules and evidentiary rules to remain mute on anything related to a client's past activities, particularly since he wasn't involved in them? Finally, discuss what exactly this mail fraud crime is, that becomes the curious solution to Mitch's problem. Perhaps you could search Westlaw® and see if the movie's claims are accurate.

Key Scene—While being chased by the firm's killers through Memphis, the head of the Morolto crime family arrives from Chicago intent on straightening out the Bendini partners who can't keep their new lawyer in line. After fending off the thugs trying to kill him, Mitch makes a surprise visit to Morolto's hotel suite. The mobster is even more surprised by Mitch's reason for the visit than Mitch's arrival, because Mitch is there to talk about overbilling. Mitch tells Morolto about the years of his firm's padding their bills, and how he has been involved with the government's investigation. Mitch just needs the client waivers—including Morolto's—to release the bills to the government. Mitch states that the billing records will not show any of the crime family's illegal activities, and, realizing his precarious situation, Mitch implies a threat to Morolto. To explain how the rules of attorney-client confidentiality require that he can never disclose any of the Morolto information beyond the billing records, Mitch looks the mobster in the face and says, "I am exactly like a ship carrying a cargo that will never reach port…as long as I'm alive."

Discussion Suggestion—Discuss the specifics of the ethics duty of client confidentiality, and how they could apply their jurisdiction's confidentiality rule to that scene. Does the duty of client confidentiality really apply in perpetuity? How does the duty of client confidentiality apply to paralegals?

FRACTURE (R; 2007)

Key Themes: Legal strategies and the double jeopardy clause, *pro se* representation, prosecutorial ethics

Best Classroom Use: Criminal Law, Criminal Procedure, Constitutional Law, Legal Ethics

113 minutes   (strong language, violence)
Cast: Anthony Hopkins, Ryan Gosling, Davis Strathairn, Rosamund Pike

Anthony Hopkins's Oscar-winning career includes a myriad of characters, both historical and fictional. But he likely will be most remembered as Hannibal Lector, the evil and psychotic killer engaged in a battle of wits with Clarice Starling, a younger but equally erudite opponent, played successively by Jodie Foster and Julianne Moore. In *Fracture*, Hopkins reprises that kind of role, that of the senior slayer attempting to one-up a junior law-enforcer—this time Ryan Gosling—and, as always, he relishes the cat-and-mouse game almost more than the victory.

Ted Crawford (Hopkins) has it all: He's an aerospace titan who drives a $600,000 Porsche to and from work, has a trophy wife, and even finds time to make the coolest Rube-Goldberg, rolling marble art pieces this side of a Dr. Seuss book, which might explain why his wife has found time for a boyfriend. The hook to her affair is that neither she nor her boyfriend knows the other's name, although the same can't be said for Crawford, who has been keeping tabs. You think someone would have noticed his car. Regardless, he establishes his moral superiority by confronting his wife's infidelity just before shooting her in the head in their gorgeous home, discharging his weapon a few more times through a window, calling the police and confessing, and waiting for the hostage negotiator. Crawford knows that the negotiator who arrives and enters Crawford's home is the boyfriend of his brain-dead wife, and during the confusion that ensues when the boyfriend realizes who is on the floor, Crawford switches his weapon with the officer's. Curious how Crawford knew what weapon his wife's boyfriend carried.

The other necessary character in *Fracture* is Willy Beachum (Gosling), who, despite being a young and broke, up-and-coming L.A. prosecutor, has a bit in common with the seasoned, murderous billionaire. Both are ambitious, brash, and sure about being the smartest guy in the room, and both love German cars (Beachum drives an old BMW 2002, widely recognized as the first sports sedan). At the time he is called to take the Crawford murder case, Beachum is on his way out the door of the District Attorney's office, having secured a new position at a high-powered, high-rise L.A. law firm, to the chagrin of the District Attorney. Wearing a tuxedo in court—because he is heading to an opera with his new and stunning female boss at the big firm—Beachum catches the eye of Crawford, who not only fires his lawyer so he can represent himself, but asks for an expedited case so he can go to trial against Beachum before it's too late.

Normally, a *pro se* defendant in an attempted murder trial is like the one-legged man in a foot race: standing up only at the start. But Crawford brings real genius to the defense counsel's table and has more than a few tricks up his sleeve, including knowing that the lead government witness—the man who was sleeping with Crawford's wife and took Crawford's confession—has yet to divulge his connection to the victim. And, no one has found the murder weapon—or what would be the murder weapon if Crawford's wife would slip from her coma. Beachum is too caught up in the anticipation of his new life and his budding lust-fest with the woman who is to help shape his new career in private practice, to realize that this open and shut case is neither. While toying with Beachum (in a manner slightly reminiscent of *Silence of the Lambs*), Crawford gets the moment he's been waiting for at trial, which results in his winning his motion for an acquittal.

It doesn't take a rocket scientist, even one like Crawford, to realize that the humiliated Beachum will throw away his chance at real money in private practice for a shot at professional redemption. But Beachum needs his old job back, he needs to find the missing gun, and he needs to find any precedent that would allow him to charge Crawford again. There is that little thing called the double jeopardy clause. Oh, and a fresh confession would be nice.

Key Scene—At the trial, Beachum establishes the key facts of the almost-murder, including the arresting cop's testimony, when Crawford finally objects to the testimony on the grounds of unlawful carnal knowledge with the victim. All hell then breaks loose, culminating in a meeting with the judge in chambers, where each side argues about whether Crawford's confession should be thrown out, and whether the fruit of the poisonous tree doctrine applies in such a macabre situation. Despite Beachum's best efforts, the judge grants Crawford's motion for acquittal.

Discussion Suggestion—Was Crawford's confession actually made under duress, under the theory that he made it in fear of the officer who took it because that officer had been sleeping with the victim? Does it matter if Crawford knew all along that his wife was having an affair with that officer? What actually is the fruit of the poisonous tree doctrine?

Key Scene—Part of the above-described includes the compromised officer offering to plant evidence in the case, telling Beachum it has to be done or else Crawford will get away with murder, almost. Beachum goes along with the plan far enough to have his secretary on call to help in the ruse if Beachum feels it's necessary. At the moment of truth, however, Beachum doesn't offer the fake evidence.

Discussion Suggestion—Is Beachum's conduct legal or even ethical? Hasn't he committed a crime by agreeing to plant evidence in a criminal case? Wouldn't this type of behavior, although not taken to fruition, be in serious violation of his jurisdiction's legal ethics rules?

Key Scene—After Crawford is granted an acquittal, he—as his comatose wife's guardian—takes his wife off life support, over the pained and frenetic counter-attempts by Beachum. While contemplating how to bring Crawford to justice, knowing that Crawford has been granted an acquittal for attempted murder, Beachum engages in legal research and the camera shows him looking at a case, *People v. Bivens*. Then, Beachum and Crawford have their verbal showdown at Crawford's house, where Crawford again confesses to shooting his wife, thinking he's protected by the double jeopardy clause. Beachum reminds him that the acquittal was for attempted murder, and now that the wife has died, things have changed.

Discussion Suggestion—There is such a California case! It is nearly on point to the key plot conflict in *Fracture*, and its citation is *People v. Bivens*, 231 Cal.App.3d 653, 282 Cal.Rptr. 438. Decided in 1991 by the California Court of Appeals, the case involved a teenage defendant who pled guilty to a brutal robbery and battery, while the attempted murder charge against him was dismissed in exchange for the plea bargain. When the victim died, the defendant was charged and convicted of murder. On appeal, the court concluded that the double jeopardy clause didn't apply to a murder charge when the victim was still alive during the attempted murder prosecution. You could have your students find the case and check the headnotes for your jurisdiction's view of the same issue, or they could argue why the double jeopardy clause should bar a murder prosecution under the facts in *Fracture*.

INTOLERABLE CRUELTY (PG-13; 2003)

Key Themes: Divorce law and prenuptial agreements, the use of lawyers for revenge, cutthroat legal tactics

Best Classroom Use: Family Law, Legal Ethics, Litigation

100 minutes   (strong language, sexual situations)

Cast: George Clooney, Catherine Zeta-Jones, Billy Bob Thornton, Edward Herrmann, Geoffrey Rush, Cedric the Entertainer

Often in legal films, an unwitting client (which means relatively honest) is eaten for lunch by a surreptitious and cunning lawyer, someone we know is the shark, not because of the sharpened teeth, but because the attack shocks no one but the prey. We all saw it coming, but, of course, we're not the seal puppy. *Intolerable Cruelty* twists this premise inside out and the shark becomes the prey. He should have seen it coming; he knows how the hunt goes down. Love is blind, though.

George Clooney is, once more, protagonist and foil, in another film made by the legendary Coen brothers. These brothers have a fondness for brutal comedies like *Raising Arizona, O Brother Where Art Thou, Fargo* (Oscar winner for Best Screenplay), *Burn after Reading*, heart-pounding film noirs like *Blood Simple*, and made the best modern western ever, *No Country for Old Men* (Oscar winner for Best Director and Best Picture). Clooney plays Miles Massey, an L.A. divorce lawyer of such renown that the mention of his name causes ulcers. The self-absorbed, marriage-loathing, Shakespeare-quoting attorney can convince a cheating spouse caught in the act that it wasn't his or her fault, and he has a prenuptial agreement that is so ironclad it bears his name: the "Massey Prenup."

One of Massey's clients is real estate developer Rex Rexroth (Edward Herrmann), a man with a penchant for trains and young women (in that order). His trophy wife Marilyn (played effortlessly by Catherine-Zeta Jones) is quick to her husband's shenanigans, and with the help of a foul-mouthed private investigator (Cedric the Entertainer), videotapes the train conductor in the act. Upon first sight of the sublime Marilyn Rexroth, Massey is smitten, to the extent someone in his line of work and with his ego can be. But his infatuation doesn't interfere with his duty to his client, culminating in a surprise attack on Mrs. Rexroth at the divorce hearing that proves she was not so much a put-upon wife of an older cheating lout, but a gold-digger in waiting who finally found her chump. Left with nothing except the sympathies of her divorced-but-rich friends, Marilyn Rexroth promises to get back at Massey and find another loaded and future ex-husband.

Things are never what they seem in a Coen brothers production. So when Marilyn arrives at Massey's office a few months later with her new fiancé, an oil tycoon (Billy Bob Thornton), looking to hire Massey for the use of his prenup to protect the tycoon's assets from Marilyn, all of us—Massey especially—should think of the Bard who wrote of scheming women and the rottenness of Denmark. Invited to the wedding, Massey watches Billy Bob Thornton (who actually knows a thing or five about divorce) eat the Massey Prenup with some barbecue sauce. With that, the chum is thrown into the sea. After her second divorce and a not-so-coincidental run-in with Massey in Vegas, where he is there to give a keynote address to a national divorce lawyers group, Marilyn tosses more bait Massey's way and his porcelain-teeth-lined-mouth opens wide. Off to a wedding chapel they go in the middle of the night. So beset with what heretofore has been unknown to him, true love, Massey insists on signing his eponymous prenup, believing he is the poorer spouse-to-be and to prove that he has no designs for Marilyn's oil-soaked divorce millions. When she rips it up, the hook is set. One less shark.

It would be too straight and narrow for the Coens to end this farce with Massey discovering he's been duped by a woman who is still broke and will now make him her third, and finally successful, divorce. Much too easy. Massey takes out a hit on his beloved bride, hiring a hit man in desperate need of an inhaler, and then frantically tries to cancel the contract after he discovers that his wife—if she stays alive long enough—will be superrich after one of her prior ex's wills is probated. Without the Massey Prenup, he will get from Marilyn what she's been vengefully scheming to get from him. But Massey gets to the hit man after Marilyn discovers the murderous plan and doubles what Wheezy Joe the hit man was being paid to kill her. Surviving divorce just became more likely than surviving marriage. The dialogue in *Intolerable Cruelty* is pitter-patter smart and funny, and reminiscent of a bygone slapstick era, without the innuendo. As usual, Clooney is terrific, willing to be the handsome fool and look the part too.

Key Scene—The film's prologue and first scene are interrupted by the opening credits, but together they make for a fun vignette about the nature of a divorce lawyer's poetic license with a client's facts. The prologue opens with a daytime television producer arriving unexpectedly early at his Hollywood Hills home, to the sound of strange noises upstairs, only to find his younger wife awkwardly explaining why the pool boy's van is in the driveway. Not having a pool can make those explanations even more awkward. Upon the paramour's entrance from the bathroom, there is no doubt he wasn't in there to measure for a hot tub. A nasty fight, both physical and verbal, ensues between husband and wife, but it was the wife who started it. She gives her husband quite the beat-down and he even photographs his injuries as she takes off in his Jaguar. When the wife visits Miles Massey seeking representation, Massey's summary of what she told him is so hilariously shaded that she has to correct her own lawyer's lies. But he convinces her that she was the injured party and that he will make her husband pay.

Discussion Section—Students could discuss or be assigned to research whether it makes any legal difference in their jurisdiction who was cheating on whom. Does current case law show that courts care about infidelity in a no-fault divorce country? As to Miles Massey's recitation of her version of events, you could discuss when lawyers have gone from shading the truth to crossing it out. Is Massey the kind of lawyer anyone should have, or just those who can afford him?

Key Scene— Massey meets with Rex Rexroth and discovers his client has no prenup. After meeting the luminous Mrs. Rexroth at a divorce negotiation held at his office, Massey is obviously smitten. For reasons that become clear in a later scene, but necessary for this key scene, Massey wines and dines Marilyn at a fancy restaurant, where they engage in flirtatious swordplay, all without the presence of Massey's client or Marilyn's lawyer. At one point while Massey is cajoling her about the divorce, Marilyn tells him that she could have him disbarred.

Discussion Section—Ask the class what is wrong in this scene and see if students notice that the whole scene, not just where Marilyn threatens disbarment, is a violation of the anticontact rule. If your students have completed a legal ethics course, then hopefully they caught that. Now, suppose he just wanted to have dinner with her for purely personal reasons. Would that be okay?

Key Scene—The day after Miles and Marilyn marry at a Vegas wedding chapel, he discovers that he's been set up and that Marilyn's marriage and divorce from the oil tycoon was literally an act. The torn-up prenup comes to mind, and soon enough, Marilyn Rexroth Doyle Massey is heading to the divorce she's made her life goal. Miles then plans a hit on his wife, which he then tries to stop mid-stream because he discovers that Rex Rexroth has died in the night, leaving his fortune to his ex-wife, who he never removed from his will following their divorce. Much hilarity and a little death ensue.

Discussion Section—Skipping over the whole ethics business of a lawyer hiring a hit man to kill his wife, focus on the family law aspects of this scene. If California is a community property state, and Miles and Marilyn have been married barely long enough for the ink on the marriage license to dry, then how much peril is Miles really in? What would their community estate be? Also, you could have your students research in your jurisdiction what the consequences actually are when a testator dies before changing his or her will to disinherit an ex-spouse.

JAGGED EDGE (R; 1985)

Key Themes: Murder trial, ethics violations, lawyer-client involvement
Best Classroom Use: Criminal Law, Legal Ethics, Litigation

108 minutes   (sexual scenes, violence)
Cast: Jeff Bridges, Glenn Close, Peter Coyote

A few years before terrorizing Michael Douglas in *Fatal Attraction*, Glenn Close costarred in this movie as a lawyer who agrees to represent a super-rich newspaper publisher accused of brutally murdering his wife. Set in San Francisco, this is more of a B-movie whodunit rather than a legal movie, although a few of the legal scenes can be used effectively in class.

Jack Forrester (Jeff Bridges) soon becomes the suspect in his wife's sadistic murder, in no small measure because he will be inheriting her publishing fortune, and because a witness claims to have seen a hunting knife—the kind evidently used in the killing—in Forrester's gym locker. Forrester's corporate lawyer realizes Forrester should have a criminal lawyer and suggests Teddy Barnes (Glenn Close), a corporate associate in the firm who left the prosecutor's office four years earlier. Teddy wants nothing to do with criminal law (for reasons we later learn), but has to meet with Forrester because her senior partner requires her. Begrudgingly, Teddy agrees only to take the case if she believes Forrester is innocent, which she soon does.

The prosecutor is not only a Senate candidate whose San Francisco Times editorial page has occasionally been pilloried, but is a former boss of Teddy, and whose unethical behavior is the reason Teddy left the prosecutor's office. Teddy is also complicit in this past indiscretion, but whatever guilt she feels doesn't stop her from another lapse in professional judgment, as she begins an affair with her client who just might be guilty of murdering his wife. The affair itself is classroom discussion material, without the need for a scene of it to be shown. As the trial unfolds, Teddy realizes that Forrester has not been honest with her, and she has a crisis of conscious about whether to pull out of the case. She decides to continue the representation, which becomes a decision she'll regret more than sleeping with her client. Along with the clues and red herrings, the film is sprinkled with a few gaffes, including one where Glenn Close wears two different suits in the same courtroom scene.

Key Scene—Soon after the murder, the prosecutor and a few of his police officers repeatedly question Forrester in the presence of his corporate lawyer. They ask Forrester if he and his wife ever fought, and after the gym locker attendant claims to have seen a knife in Forrester's locker, whether he ever hunted or owns a hunting knife. After denying owning a hunting knife, Forrester is arrested.

Discussion Suggestion—You shouldn't even need a prompter for this scene. You should be questioning why any lawyer would allow his or her client under suspicion for murder to talk to the police or prosecutor. In reality, how could this come back to haunt a defendant?

Key Scene—Early in the trial, Teddy is cross-examining the victim's brother, and asks him if he believes Forrester is the murderer. "God, no" the brother responds, to which the prosecutor objects without stating his reason, and the judge sustains the objection. Then, a close friend of the victim is called to the stand and the prosecutor asks her about what the victim had told the friend about the state of her marriage to Forrester. Now Teddy objects, claiming that such testimony is hearsay. The prosecutor responds that this testimony goes to the state of the victim's mind and is an allowable exception, to which the judge agrees. The friend then tells the jury that the victim had discussed divorcing Forrester.

Discussion Suggestion—What would be the prosecutor's reason for objecting to Teddy's question? Is it a realistic objection? How would the hearsay rule and its exceptions affect the desired testimony about what the victim allegedly told her friend about the state of the marriage?

LEGAL EAGLES (PG; 1986)

Key Themes: Prosecutorial and defense misconduct, ethics, murder trial
Best Classroom Use: Legal Ethics, Criminal Law

116 minutes   (strong language, provocative situation)
Cast: Robert Redford, Debra Winger, Daryl Hannah, Brian Dennehy, Terence Stamp

A harmless mystery/criminal procedure drama/romantic comedy that tries too hard to be all things to all people, *Legal Eagles* pairs Robert Redford and Debra Winger as opposing attorneys in a criminal case with Daryl Hannah at the center of the mystery, who is vying for the affections of one attorney and the assistance of the other. Although the legal scenes lack authenticity, they are entertaining and a few of them would work well in a legal ethics course, or even a criminal law course as teaching tools for what not to do.

Redford plays Tom Logan, an assistant district attorney in Manhattan who everyone—including his boss, the D.A.—believes should be the next candidate for District Attorney. Redford needs no method acting here to play a strikingly handsome, well-spoken, and sharply dressed man on the move. His confidence in the courtroom is such that he talks to the jury directly and inappropriately, but refuses the grant of a mistrial, claiming that he "trusts this jury, your honor." While speaking at a legal society banquet one night, Logan is interrupted by publicity seeking defense attorney Laura Kelley (Debra Winger) and her beautiful client, Chelsea Deardon (Daryl Hannah), an ethereal performance artist. Deardon has been charged with attempting to steal the only surviving painting left by her dead father, whose fiery death was witnessed by the much younger Chelsea at the film's opening. Attorney Kelley believes that if Logan could just hear the reasons behind the alleged theft attempt, he would not only drop the charges against Chelsea, but would investigate the owner of the painting for fraud, and maybe murder. According to Chelsea, she didn't attempt to steal the painting because it was already hers, given to her by her father on her eighth birthday and bearing his well wishes to her on the back of the canvas. According to Chelsea, the man who owns the painting stole it from her when he and an art dealer conspired to kill her father years earlier.

This film has one thing in common with a Hitchcock thriller: the McGuffin. Essentially, a McGuffin is a plot element that is needed only to create tension between the characters or to drive the narrative. The McGuffin need not to be accurate or even explained for the film to succeed, and Hitchcock used it in films like *Notorious, North by Northwest*, and *Psycho*. For example, a spy might be sent to find a key map in another country without the viewer needing to know what the map is or why it is important to the spy's bosses. And for *Legal Eagles*, the McGuffin is the art fraud conspiracy that Chelsea says is the reason behind her father's death and the criminal events that take place throughout the film. None of it makes sense, but it drives the film through its legal elements.

Here is where the movie enters the consciousness for our purposes. Tom Logan does that which we suspect he might: After getting too comfortable with defense attorney Kelley and working with her to investigate her client Chelsea's claim, he sleeps with Chelsea, someone he is supposed to be prosecuting. This rendezvous gets him fired. But he isn't unemployed for long, thanks to the job offer of his former opponent. So, in a matter of minutes, the former prosecutor is now sharing office space with Kelley as they work together to defend Chelsea, a less than honest client with a penchant for showing up where people are about to die. There are a few interesting courtroom scenes in *Legal Eagles,* but unfortunately, the film has more fireworks outside the courtroom than in it.

Key Scene—After seeing art dealer Taft (Terence Stamp), Chelsea heads to Logan's apartment for comfort, claiming that someone is following her. Against his better judgment, Logan lets Chelsea stay the night, a night that includes them sharing a bed. Logan's affair with the woman he is to be prosecuting is immediately discovered and after a heated exchange with the District Attorney, Logan is fired. Chelsea's defense attorney, Ms. Kelley, then reads Logan the riot act, but asks him to join her at work. The former prosecutor sets up shop with his former nemesis.

Discussion Section—Here's an easy question for your students to discuss: What in these connected scenes would *not* result in disciplinary actions against Logan and Kelley? Beyond that, would a judge allow a lawyer who yesterday was the prosecutor to be co-defense counsel the next day? Supposing the client waived the conflict of interest, would that make it allowable?

Key Scene—At the start of what has now become a murder trial, Logan makes an opening statement that asks the jury member to raise their hands if they think Chelsea is guilty. He tells them he thinks she is and they begin raising their hands, at the outrage of the prosecutor. As the judge attempts to declare a mistrial, Logan protests, telling the judge that he believes in the jury's integrity and wants to continue.

Discussion Section—Would a lawyer be allowed to overrule a judge's conclusion on a mistrial? Assuming a mistrial, would Logan be allowed to continue to represent Chelsea, or has he committed legal malpractice?

Key Scene—While trying to get proof of the insurance fraud that would prove Chelsea's innocence (assuming anyone could follow the theory), Logan and Kelley assume the identities of claims adjustors in order to get a box of insurance files they need. Deft deception helps Logan get what he needs.

Discussion Section—Wouldn't they be able to get those files through traditional discovery? Assuming that the film didn't end in such an explosive fashion, would that evidence have been admissible at trial?

LIAR LIAR (PG-13; 1997)

Key Themes: Lawyer dishonesty, law office politics, marital property distribution
Best Classroom Use: Introduction to Paralegal Studies, Legal Ethics, Family Law, Contracts

87 minutes   (strong language, provocative situation)
Cast: Jim Carrey, Maura Tierney, Jennifer Tilly, Amanda Donohoe, Jason Bernard, Justin Cooper

Even though many lawyers are sensitive about their public perception as conniving sharks, this fanciful yarn is likely to insult no one. *Liar Liar's* high jinks about a lawyer forced to tell the truth for 24 hours isn't a morality tale, but a fun look at the perils of being completely honest, set in a legal environment.

Fletcher Reede (Jim Carrey) would be the attorney we all would hate, if it weren't for his boyish charm. He lies to everyone about everything, from telling a coworker he likes her struck-by-lightning hairstyle, to having his secretary tell his mom he is sick so he doesn't have to talk with her, to telling his little son Max (Jason Cooper) he missed his birthday party because of an unexpected case emergency. His emergency is more personal than professional, because after eagerly agreeing to take a divorce client (Jennifer Tilly) when another lawyer in the firm refuses to lie about the facts, Fletcher sleeps with his boss Miranda (Amanda Donohoe), hoping that will increase his chances of making partner. Max, already missing his divorced father and having had enough of the lies, takes matters into his own hands and makes a birthday cake wish that his dad would have to tell the truth for 24 hours. After Fletcher wakes up from his tryst with his boss, he is shocked—and smacked—upon realizing he can no longer tell a lie.

Fletcher's honesty problem affects him everywhere he goes: on an elevator with a neighbor who wonders why everyone is so nice to her, on the street with a police officer who asks Fletcher if he knows why he was pulled over, and at his office with his colleagues who want to know what he really thinks of them. But, the most pressing consequence of his inability to lie involves his trollop of a client's chance of nullifying her prenuptial agreement, which has a steep penalty for infidelity. Even though her adulterous activities are well established, Fletcher thought he could lie his way out of it during the hearing, at least before his son's wish came true. Now that Fletcher is incapable of being anything but brutally honest, he must resort to a new strategy, which is to seek a continuance. When that fails, he has no choice to but to go on the attack—against his client. Somehow, that works, and the prenuptial agreement is declared void, to Fletcher's dismay. But all's well that ends well, and Fletcher and Max are reunited on account of Max's fateful wish.

Key Scene—After being possessed by honesty, Fletcher is back at the office as his secretary is getting ready to quit. On the phone, Fletcher tells a criminal defense client of his to "Stop breaking the law, asshole!" Soon, he is hustled into a partners meeting by his boss Miranda, who hopes that his unabated honesty will get him fired, as she has asked him what he thinks of those sitting around the conference table. He riffs nastily on the senior partner and is flabbergasted to realize that the partner finds it a needed dose of levity at the stuffy firm. Then, the partner tells Fletcher to give the business to everyone and, by the end, all the partners are in stitches with laughter and Miranda is chagrined.

Discussion Suggestion—This scene is a good segue into a discussion of law office politics and how treacherous it can be to discuss your coworkers and supervisors with them, much less be intimately involved with them. If you work in a legal environment, discuss what you have seen of office politics and its pitfalls.

Key Scene—In court to get his client as much of her ex-husband's money as possible, Fletcher must convince the judge that his client didn't commit adultery, in violation of the prenuptial agreement, despite the crystal clear evidence to the contrary. When that proves futile, Fletcher's honesty and panic lead him stumbling across quite a fact, namely that his client lied about her age when getting married. Doing some quick extrapolation, Fletcher argues that under California law, since his client was actually 17 when she signed the prenuptial agreement, she would have needed her parents' consent to enter into such a contract. Therefore, the prenuptial agreement is void, and she is entitled to community property rights. The judge agrees with Fletcher's position.

Discussion Suggestion—This scene could be used in both Family Law and Contracts, as it involves prenuptial agreement nullification and the voidability of minors' contracts. Can a minor make a valid prenuptial agreement? Does someone who has been an adult for years lose the right to disaffirm a contract made while a minor? Finally, what is community property all about?

THE LIFE OF DAVID GALE (R; 2003)

Key Themes: The death penalty, miscarriage of justice, ends justifying the means
Best Classroom Use: Criminal Law, Introduction to Law

131 minutes   (nudity, sexual situations, strong language, graphic death scene)
Cast: Kevin Spacey, Laura Linney, Kate Winslet, Gabriel Mann

When does satire become demagoguery, cross over into caricature, and then jump headlong into hilariously preposterous? Watch *The Life of David Gale* and find out. Although this movie is quite entertaining, it tries so hard to show how evil the death penalty is that it unintentionally makes a pro death penalty argument. And yet, it deserves a viewing, if for no other reason than to stir the passions about capital punishment.

Kate Winslet plays Bitsey Bloom, an investigative journalist so loyal to her subjects that she served a jail sentence for refusing to give up a sexual predator. Because of this journalistic integrity, she is chosen by David Gale (Kevin Spacey), a convicted murderer who wants her to interview him three days in a row before his scheduled execution at the end of the week. Bitsey's employer agrees to pay $500,000 dollars to Gale for the access, and much of the film is presented in flashbacks. Dr. David Gale, a philosophy professor at the University of Texas with a penchant for the student body, is one of the nation's most charismatic and vocal anti-death penalty advocates. His best friend is Constance (Laura Linney), a colleague and fellow member of "Death Watch," a national anti-death penalty group who engages in protests and debates with politicians.

Then, David Gale is accused of raping a student, and his wife leaves him, taking their little boy with her. He loses his job as a result of this indiscretion and no other university will hire him, despite the charges having been dropped. When Constance is raped and murdered in her home, David Gale is summarily arrested and convicted, no doubt because the physical evidence found in and on Constance is his. So, days before this crusader against capital punishment gets executed in the nation's leading death penalty state, Gale tells Bitsey his story, hoping she'll accomplish in three days what his lawyer and he couldn't in the prior years – find out how he was framed. What seems unsettling about these interviews is that David Gale seems resigned to his fate, as if his ending is more preordained than his unjust conviction.

Bitsey's interviews do little to change her view on Gale's guilt, until she finds a video tape hanging in her motel room which shows a nude Constance in the last minutes of her life, a snuff film that has to be the work of the real killer. As Bitsey hurriedly digs deeper into this mystery, several theories materialize about who Constance's killer is, and a second videotape is found hours before Gale's execution which provides undeniable proof that Constance, suffering from a terminal illness, killed herself. The thesis of this movie is that the death penalty is not only immoral and barbaric, but wrong on its face in that the innocent are sometimes executed. Such a view is held by many credible Americans and lawyers, including famed O.J. Simpson lawyer and Innocence Project co-founder, Barry Scheck, as well as Scott Turow, who wrote a serious essay on the subject, the book *Ultimate Punishment*.

At this point, a SPOILER ALERT must be given. If you haven't seen this movie, then you should skip the next paragraph and go to the key scene portion.

After Gale is executed for a murder he didn't commit, Bitsey comes into possession of a third video, sent to her by the key principals, which shows what really happened: David Gale was actually involved in and present at Constance's grotesque suicide. All of this was done in order to prove that an innocent man can be executed.

Key Scene—The evening after having sex with the coed who will later accuse him of rape, David Gale and Texas's governor appear together on a political affairs show to debate the death penalty. Although the scene is slanted to make the governor look like a Bible thumping cretin, there are interesting arguments exchanged. And, knowing the movie's conclusion makes watching the governor challenge Gale to name any innocent Texan ever executed all the more ironic and heavy-handed.

Discussion Suggestion—Naturally, you also could debate the death penalty after watching this scene, analyzing the arguments presented, and providing your own pros and cons.

Michael Clayton (R; 2007)

Key Themes: Corporate criminality, civil litigation, litigator guilt, law firm politics
Best Classroom Use: Litigation, Business Law, Criminal Law, Legal Ethics

116 minutes   (strong language, violence)
Cast: George Clooney, Tom Wilkinson, Tilda Swinton, Sidney Pollack

Guilt has a way of finding its own gap and forcing an escape, despite all preventative measures to keep it captive. For Lady Macbeth, guilt drove her to madness, and for Macbeth it was sleeplessness. And so it is with *Michael Clayton*, a film that reaches greatness, that the author who penned, "First let's kill all the lawyers," might only have to say now, "There's no need to. They're doing just fine on their own." So outstanding are the performances and the key scenes in this Oscar-nominated film that one overlooks the triteness of its driving message: Huge corporations are evil and big law firms get paid blood money to keep the secrets buried by bulldozers driven by their best litigators.

Three lawyers are unraveling in *Michael Clayton*. The first is the lawyer you never want to face in court, Arthur Edens (Tom Wilkinson). He is the best there is at the Manhattan powerhouse firm of Kenner, Bach & Ledeen, and he's been representing U-North, an international agriculture conglomerate, in a class-action case for the last 30,000 billable hours. The plaintiffs are small farmers who claim that U-North's fertilizer called Culcitate is killing them. At a deposition in Milwaukee, Arthur can no longer repress his guilt and has a mental breakdown, culminating in him stripping naked in front of a teenage plaintiff and expressing his love for her. Not a good idea. Worse yet, Arthur's insanity seems permanent and brought on by the realization that he has spent much of his working years covering up the crimes of his client, just for millions in legal fees. For him, lucidity now means making amends.

The second lawyer is U-North's too-tightly wound general counsel Karen Crowder (Tilda Swinton). She has been working at the company for well over a decade, rising to her current position, all the while knowing that a big company has to break some eggs if it wants to make omelets. But Arthur's meltdown causes Crowder to do things and have things ordered done so a settlement in this forever-case can be quickly had. Things that are so unsettling she begins profusely sweating and fracturing in front of our eyes. Tilda Swinton more than earned her Oscar for best supporting actress.

The third lawyer is the eponymous Michael Clayton (George Clooney), who's been dispatched to Milwaukee to bring Edens home and get him back on track, as it were. Michael Clayton has worked at Kenner, Bach & Leeden for 17 years and is so far from being a partner he's known as the firm's janitor. Say your client's maid needs a jump to the front of the INS line; suppose your client's son got a DUI on spring break that won't look good on his law school application; suppose your kleptomaniac client has been caught stealing. Have Clayton get his hands dirty cleaning the mess and keep your own law license secure. He's a man at the horns of a dilemma: By securing the silence of his good and crazy friend (who is now helping the plaintiffs) so that a settlement can be struck and the massive tort case put to bed, Clayton knows he will be out of work. The settlement will help Kenner, Bach & Leeden avoid a malpractice claim against their best and now bewildering litigator, and it will be able to finalize its merger with an even larger law firm. Clayton's services will no longer be needed because his boss and senior partner (Sidney Pollack, in his last role) will be retiring on his merger-money. Beyond that, Clayton's Plan B for his future, a bar he started with his loser-brother, has gone belly-up and Clayton needs $75,000 in a week to pay off the remaining debts to his creditors. And they're not bankers. Clayton's efforts for his firm in the next few days, whether successful or not, will for him result in the same ending. Loss. He is terminal, yet has no other choice but to forge ahead because he can't afford, nor has the time, for a meltdown. Henry Thoreau would have spotted the quiet desperation in Clayton's eyes

The lives of these three lawyers will intersect into a deadly braid over a four-day period. The first lawyer seeks to undo the damage he believes he's caused in the name of money. The second lawyer makes ever-more-brutal decisions for the good of the company balance sheet. The third lawyer just tries to make it through each day, knowing that every step forward will take him back to where he has no future, especially if he's killed along the way. Without question, *Michael Clayton* is worth a full viewing in class, but some key scenes will suffice in a few classes.

Key Scene—Early in the film, Clayton is called by a lawyer at Kenner, Bach & Leeden to make a midnight run to West Chester where one of the lawyer's high-dollar clients has just committed hit-and-run. This scene will appear again in the pivotal part of the movie, but for now, all we know is that Clayton is sent to clean a mess. The driver is strangely bitter at having been bothered by a jogger who hogs a road traveled by luxury cars, and while standing in his kitchen, he begins berating Michael Clayton. As the driver throws out a few poorly thought excuses to make his problem disappear, he becomes more irate at Clayton's responses and yells, "I thought you were a miracle worker." And here is where Clayton calmly utters the self-deprecating line about only being a janitor. He offers a few, immediate solutions and is on his way.

Discussion Suggestion—Students could discuss what Michael Clayton could actually do for the client that night. Why was Michael Clayton really there, and did he do anything unethical? For a research assignment, students could find what level crime hit-and-run driving in their jurisdiction is.

Key Scene—Clayton finally finds Arthur Edens back in New York City, walking in an alley with a bag bull of baguettes. Their tense reunion is punctuated by Arthur's realization that someone out there must be tapping his phone, and during the scene Clayton implies that Arthur might be institutionalized against his will. Arthur's response about New York's civil incapacity standards shows that he may be crazy, but not stupid.

Discussion Suggestion—Your students could research and then write a short memo on what in their jurisdiction is the standard for civil commitment. Is the key factor danger, as Arthur states, and is he right that evidence of criminal activity in another jurisdiction is irrelevant?

Key Scene—After Arthur's murder, Michael Clayton discovers the U-North internal memo on the deadly properties of Culcitate. Not only did Arthur have a copy of it unbeknownst to U-North, and not only did he read the key portions of it into Karen Crowder's voice mail, but he has had hundreds of copies made before his death. The memo proves that U-North was aware of that which it has been denying under oath for years.

Discussion Suggestion—This may be a bit too much for a business law class, but students could discuss if the Sarbanes-Oxley Act requires U-North's counsel to disclose the memo. In the alternative, students in a legal ethics course could discuss the propriety of making copies of internal company memoranda. Should Arthur Edens be considered a hero whistleblower, or can lawyers even be whistleblowers?

Key Scene—The last scene is so viscerally satisfying, as Karen Crowder and U-North become criminally surprised to discover that Michael Clayton is not dead. Her attempt to buy him off right in the lobby of the second floor of a hotel is all caught on tape, thanks to Michael and his other brother, the police officer.

Discussion Suggestion—First, is Crowder's claim that the internal company memo is protected by attorney-client privilege accurate? Second, would her bribe and admission, all captured by whatever wiretapping mechanism employed, be admissible? Since Michael's police officer-brother was involved, would that make Michael an agent of the government, and if so, would a search warrant be required first?

MINORITY REPORT (PG-13; 2002)

Key Themes: Preventative justice and *actus reus*, crime control and constitutional safeguards

Best Classroom Use: Criminal Law, Criminal Procedure, Introduction to Law

146 minutes   (graphic violence, drug use, strong language)
Cast: Tom Cruise, Max von Sydow, Colin Farrell, Samantha Morton, Lois Smith, Kathryn Morris

Science fiction, when done well, has that ability to provoke or frighten us about what hasn't happened yet or is unlikely to occur, but seems believable enough to keep us thinking even after we put down the novel or return the DVD. *Fahrenheit 451*, about a world where books are banned and burned for the good of the citizenry, is a classic example of the didactic heights science fiction can reach. And so is *Minority Report*, which is a triumph in the pure thriller genre, but has much more to say about the nature of predestination being controlled by technology for the greater good. The writings of science fiction author Philip K. Dick have been the source for many movies, and *Minority Report* is a derivative of a 1956 short story of his. Released less than a year after the passage of the Patriot Act, the post-9/11 antiterrorism legislation so culturally popular at the time that only one senator voted against its passage, the film version raises serious issues about the propriety of intrusive policing in the noble attempt to prevent horrible crimes.

John Anderton (Tom Cruise) is a Washington, D.C. police officer in charge of a special homicide unit called the Department of Precrime. Calling him a detective would be technically accurate, but not in the traditional sense, because in 2055 the District has been murder-free for six years. Thanks to the metaphysical and unexplainable genius of three odd teenagers connected by electrodes floating in a milky bath in the "temple" at police headquarters, these precognitives, known as "precogs," see murders before they occur. After being arrested for "premurder," the prisoner has a metal halo placed on his or her head and is put into a coma-state and placed in a futuristic prison where the prisoners stand inside lit cylinders in their vegetative state—for life.

John Anderton believes in the precrime experiment with his whole heart because his mentor boss Lamar Burgess (Max von Sydow) created it. More importantly, had the system been in place some years earlier, his own son wouldn't have been murdered. The Justice Department is considering adopting the precrime program, and a highly suspicious official (Colin Farrell) is on hand to inspect the workings of the precogs, three orphans of heavy drug users whose psychic powers are the result of *in utero* drug addiction. Then, the precogs see a murder that will be committed in 36 hours and John Anderton is shown to be the murderer of a person he has never seen before. Thus begins the chase portion of the film, as Tom Cruise runs for his life in a futuristic world of ocular laser scans and living billboards while trying to prove he couldn't and wouldn't commit the murder he has been "chosen" to commit.

What a minority report has to do with preventing John's future murder or resolving the mystery surrounding another murder, would require more exposition than is necessary here. More important than the film's dénouement is its presentation of the dilemma of how technology can be used to monitor everyone's activities so that the truly bad among us can be "caught" before they in fact commit their deeds. While perhaps unintended, the dilemma presented in *Minority Report* is similar to the conclusions that opponents of the Patriot Act have made about increased wiretapping allowances, "person of interest" labels, and the jailing of suspects without charges having to be filed. This is one of the more thought-provoking movies, scientific or otherwise, of recent years.

Key Scene—The opening scene shows the precrime division at work, furiously trying to stop a murder before it is committed. A man notices another man hanging around his neighborhood. The first man has a suspicion about his wife and leaves their house, only to hang around his own house and wait out his suspicion. Meanwhile, the precrime unit witnesses the spousal murder as it comes out of the precogs brains. It will occur in a few minutes, but the police don't know exactly where the family lives, and are trying to comb through the dreams of the precogs to get an address before it's too late. The husband's crime is averted at the last second, and he is arrested for "premurder," haloed with the brain-draining metal band, and sent to prison.

Discussion Suggestion—Upon viewing this scene, discuss what crime the husband did commit, even though no murder occurred. As the scene is presented, the precrime unit has done nothing premature at the time they arrest the husband (although their lack of due process and adjudication is shocking), and some might take the position that this scene supports the rightness of such a precrime activity.

Key Scene—At the film's climax, Police Commissioner Lamar Burgess is exposed as a treacherous culprit, and he and his protégé John Anderton have a showdown on a balcony overlooking the Washington Monument. Lamar realizes his great experiment is over, and he and John intently discuss the nature of predestination and the possibility of altered destinies. After Lamar's death, Tom Cruise's voice announces in a short narration that the precrime experiment was abandoned and that, "all prisoners were unconditionally pardoned and released, although police departments keep watch on many of them for years to come."

Discussion Suggestion—Those who paid careful attention to this scene might think, "What? Kept watch on them for many years to come? Does that mean that the precrime methods were legitimate?" It seems like the antidote to the precrime problem was the very thing that some moviegoers thought the precrime experiment was supposed to represent: The Patriot Act. Discuss the pros and cons of crime prevention in a post-9/11 America, and examine some of the more controversial parts of the Patriot Act.

MY COUSIN VINNY (R; 1992)

Key Themes: Fish out of water in the criminal justice system, wrongful accusation, mistaken identity, culture clashes
Best Classroom Use: Criminal Procedure, Criminal Law, Legal Ethics, Interviewing

120 minutes   (strong language)
Cast: Joe Pesci, Marisa Tomei, Ralph Macchio, Fred Gwynne, Mitchell Whitfield

My Cousin Vinny is a delightful legal film that is actually funny, something many other comedies are not. This fish out of water story takes place on two levels, culturally and in the courtroom. Like *Erin Brockovich, Philadelphia, To Kill a Mockingbird*, and *Wall Street*, an actor won an Oscar playing a key role. Here, it is Marisa Tomei, playing the world's most interesting—and interestingly dressed—expert witness.

While driving through Alabama, Bill Gambini (Ralph Macchio) and Stan Rothenstein (Mitchell Whitfield) stop at the roadside Sac-O-Suds for some snacks. These two New Yorkers are soon pulled over by a trooper, arrested, and taken to jail. Believing they are being charged with stealing a can of tuna, they each confess to vague questions about the murder of the store employee, which happened minutes after they left. Shocked to find himself and his friend on the fast track to being convicted of murder, Bill calls the only lawyer he knows, his cousin Vinny (Joe Pesci), from Brooklyn. Straight from central casting, Vincent La Guardia Gambini and his girlfriend Mona Lisa Vito (Marisa Tomei) talk and look as out of place in small town Alabama as the locals would be if they were plunked down in Vinny's hometown. Even worse than being out of place, Vinny is woefully inexperienced. Having recently passed the bar exam on his sixth attempt, Vinny's only cases have been personal injury, and he's never been to court. Lying about his experience to the trial judge (Fred Gwynne) in order to be granted *pro hac vice* status, and desperately in need of proper courtroom attire, Vinny soon finds himself in jail for contempt.

The prosecution's case seems open and shut. Witnesses claimed to have seen two young men meeting the defendants' descriptions leaving the Sac-O-Suds at around the same time of the murder, fleeing in a green convertible just like the one Bill was driving. And, the tire marks left at the scene perfectly match the tire tread of Bill's car. Making matters worse, if that's possible, Vinny has no idea what the rules of procedure or evidence are. But he has a few things going for him, like his Brooklyn-born street sense and quick thinking, and his sharp tongued fiancée, who will be called as the defense's key witness to testify about the difference between the tire marks left from a 1964 Buick Skylark and a 1963 Pontiac Tempest. Never has an expert witness been so succinct.

Key Scene—The prosecutor, while stern, isn't out to railroad the out-of-towner defendants, and takes a liking to Vinny Gambini, telling Vinny that the missing murder weapon is a hole in the prosecution's case, and inviting Vinny hunting. Vinny believes this bonding experience will help him to discover the prosecutor's evidence, since Vinny believes there is no other way to learn the incriminating facts. During this trip, Vinny tells the prosecutor that he would sure like to know what is in the prosecutor's case file, which prompts the prosecutor to call his secretary to tell her to send a copy of the entire file to Vinny's motel room. Upon getting back from the trip, Vinny is told by Mona Lisa, who spent the downtime looking through Vinny's criminal procedure book, that the prosecutor was required by full disclosure rules to be so generous.

Discussion Suggestion—This scene could be viewed in two parts, pausing after the point where Vinny explains to Mona Lisa why he believes it is in his best interest to go hunting with the prosecutor. Analyze what is wrong with Vinny's theory. Then, after the conclusion of the second half, research your jurisdiction's rules on a prosecutor's disclosure obligations.

Key Scene—Although there are quite a few attention-grabbing courtroom scenes with their own direct and cross-examinations, there is a short scene involving the examination of an eyewitness that would work well in class. The witness tells the jury on direct examination that he observed the defendants entering and leaving the Sac-O-Suds, which took five minutes. On cross-examination, he says he's sure of the five-minute interval between the defendants' entering and leaving the store because he was cooking his breakfast at the time, and that takes five minutes. Vinny asks the witness what he cooked for breakfast that morning. Upon hearing that the guy had grits with his eggs, Vinny pounces, knowing from his own grits introduction a few days earlier that grits cook in 15 to 20 minutes, casting doubt on that witness's testimony.

Discussion Suggestion—This scene is a great example of the value of keen listening skills, which all lawyers and paralegals should possess. Asking the witness what he had for breakfast is a probe question, seeking something behind a witness's answers. Probe questions can't be prepared in advance, so a sharp paralegal uses his or her listening skills as Vinny did, to pan for gold.

Nuts (R; 1987)

Key Themes: Competence to stand trial, killing in self-defense, sexual abuse
Best Classroom Use: Criminal Procedure, Criminal Law, Interviewing

116 minutes   (strong language, rape scene)
Cast: Barbra Streisand, Richard Dreyfuss, Karl Malden, Maureen Stapleton, Eli
               Wallach, James Whitmore, Leslie Nielsen

Based on a play by the same name, *Nuts* is a hard-edged courtroom drama about mental competence and sexual abuse that gives Barbra Streisand the chance to do what she does best: be Barbra Streisand. Although she doesn't sing in the film or on the soundtrack, she provides all the smart-alecking and emoting of *Funny Girl, The Way We Were,* and *Yentl*, minus the outfits and scenery.

In a typically overcrowded New York City criminal courtroom, a judge is trying to move case files from one side of his desk to the other. One of the female defendants waiting to hear her name called is Claudia Draper (Barbra Streisand), whose parent are sitting in the gallery with an expensive lawyer they've hired for her. Claudia's disdain for the lawyer is only exceeded by the palpable enmity she has for her mother (Maureen Stapleton) and stepfather (Karl Malden). The reason the family has gathered that morning is that Claudia, a pricey call-girl, has been charged with first-degree manslaughter after stabbing her last client (Leslie Nielsen) in the neck with a shard from her bathroom mirror. The issue for the judge is whether Claudia is competent to stand trial for a charge for which self-defense is obvious. If Claudia isn't competent, she'll be committed to an institution for the criminally insane for at least a year, and then re-evaluated.

Amazingly, everyone except Claudia, from the prosecutor to Claudia's parents and their lawyer, everyone, wants her declared incompetent, a determination that seems more likely after Claudia attacks her lawyer at the start of the competency hearing. Nearby in the courtroom is Aaron Levinsky (Dreyfuss), a legal aid lawyer who the judge picks to be the next nose for Claudia to break. Levinsky can neither afford to add her to his client list nor refuse the judge's order. What ensues is a hapless lawyer with a few days and no resources to prepare his catatonic and volcanic client for a competency hearing. Even if you haven't seen this movie before, you likely can surmise why this upper-middle-class girl grew up to be a prostitute who hates her mother and seethes at the sight of her stepfather, and who sketches childlike drawings of families with no mouths on their faces.

Levinsky proves that in almost every legal movie, a legal aid lawyer is better than the prosecuting attorney. That Levinsky would suffer the abuses of being the overworked and underpaid lawyer at the bottom of the food chain, all the while being the most capable counsel in the courtroom, would seem to make him crazier than his client. Much of the courtroom scenes focus on issues less related to her ability to understand the charges (which is good, because she clearly does understand them) and more as to the motivations behind her sexual history and parental rage. *Nuts* has some compelling scenes and in a large sense questions the concept of normalcy, but one is left wondering why the prosecutor and Claudia's first lawyer (who had never before met her) would insist from the outset that she be declared incompetent.

Key Scene—After Levinksy is appointed to represent Claudia, he conducts his initial client interview in the bowels of the jail's psychiatric ward. The interview takes its natural course: Levinsky is first nonplussed and then annoyed at his client's demeanor and difficulty; Claudia is scatterbrained, overtly sexual, and nearly violent. She tries to convince Levinsky that no shrinks are needed to prove her sanity because she can do it all by herself if she gets to testify at the competency hearing.

Discussion Section—If shown in an interviewing course, students could discuss how a legal professional can effectively deal with a difficult client. What in Claudia's body language and answers indicate to an interviewer that there is more to the story than that she is "crazy?" How did Levinsky use his listening skills and questioning techniques to gather key information from a noncompliant interviewee?

Key Scene—At the competency hearing, the state's psychiatrist is called to testify about his dealings with Claudia and what had led him to conclude that she was incompetent. In this scene, the standard of competency is stated as being that as a result of mental disease or defect, Claudia can't understand the charges against her or aid in her own defense. Levinsky strenuously cross-examines the psychiatrist, particularly his conclusion that her violence toward others and overt sexuality toward him was indicative of her incompetence. During his testimony, the psychiatrist discusses her so-called crimes.

Discussion Section—What actually is competence to stand trial, and how is it different from criminal insanity? Although the movie seems more to be about the insanity defense versus self-defense rather than the issue of competence, this scene at least forces the viewer to confront what is alleged to be a competency standard. Students could conduct a mini-research project on this scene to see if it accurately reflects the law. The federal standard for competence to stand trial is 18 U.S.C. § 4241, and it includes the standard, the proof required (preponderance of the evidence), and the consequences of being declared incompetent.

Key Scene—The stepfather is called to testify at the hearing for no other reason than to make sure he can be cross-examined and outed as the one who sexually abused a much younger Claudia, causing her promiscuity and prostitution. On direct examination, he acts like the perfect provider who stepped in when Claudia's father deserted her mother, and testifies to Claudia's ever-disintegrating state of mind. While cross-examining the stepfather, Levinsky has an epiphany and begins to peel away the layers of the stepfather's façade, resulting in a meltdown on the witness stand that includes his weeping denial/confession to Claudia. He's never seen again in the film.

Discussion Section—Assuming the worst from what was shown, could the stepfather be convicted of any crime? Have your students find the applicable statute of limitations on sexual molestation to see if any charges could be brought against him. Could Claudia still bring a civil suit against him for his horrific torts against her? As to the underlying testimony, what did it have to do with Claudia's competency, and why didn't Levinsky object to the stepfather's direct testimony? Considering the sexual abuse she suffered as a child at the hands of her stepfather, would that make Claudia more or less likely to be incompetent, or is that irrelevant to the issue?

THE PAPER CHASE (PG; 1973)

Key Themes: Law school and the stress of studying, handling enormous academic pressure, obsession with a professor

Best Classroom Use: Contracts, Introduction to Paralegal Studies, Legal Ethics

113 minutes   (strong language)
Cast: Timothy Bottoms, John Houseman, Lindsay Wagner, Edward Herrmann, James Naughton

The Paper Chase establishes that one doesn't need blood, weapons, dismembered limbs, or virgins to make a great horror film. Horror only requires that your worst fears, whatever they are, be stoked by a monster, in whatever shape it takes, whose plans for you provoke white-knuckles-terror. Here, the fear is failure and the monster is Harvard Law School's most famous and acerbic law professor.

The Paper Chase is about the trials and tribulations of first-year law students at Harvard, and it takes but a few minutes for the blood-curdling scream to be heard. The film's focus is on James Hart (Timothy Bottoms), a University of Minnesota graduate who is brilliant enough to get into Harvard Law School, and yet evidently unaware that all students are to have read the first day's reading assignment before the first class. Harvard has no new student orientation? And so, the humiliation doled out on him by Professor Charles Kingsfield (John Houseman), Harvard's sadistic master of contract law and patrician elocution, foreshadows much of what makes being a first-year law student excruciating. It's been two decades since I was in my first law school class, but watching Professor Kingsfield survey his chart of the head-shot-photos of the students sitting in their assigned seats in his Contracts class, searching for the next victim of his Socratic meat grinder, brought to mind the kind of flashbacks that require group therapy or Thorazine.

Hart's first day in law school involves meeting a few other Ivy Leaguers, who form a study group with him, each one being assigned a course to outline for the eventual final exam. Some of Hart's fellow students are the legacy kind, for whom law school at Harvard is a family heirloom, and some have the self-proclaimed photographic memory, and others are the kind of nerds F. Scott Fitzgerald referred to as Harvard "sissies" in *This Side of Paradise*. Of course, Fitzgerald was a Princeton man.

Hart's course to outline is Contracts, and with each passing class Hart becomes more and more obsessed with the estimable Kingsfield, who by the end of the semester seems to be a touch impressed with Hart's classroom participation. Although Hart is the film's protagonist, Kingsfield is its star. Jonathan Houseman (in his first major film role) won an Academy award as the legendary legal lion, and he embodies the cruel precision of the archetypal professor every law student has experienced. For me, it was Professor Kelly, and he taught...Contracts.

Coincidental with Hart's worship of Professor Kingsfield is his budding romance with Kingsfield's still-married daughter Susan (Lindsay Wagner), facts Hart comes to learn later. As the first year progresses, the study group begins to crumble, thanks to the kind of jungle pressures that cause some animals to eat their young and some to jump off cliffs. Hart wrestles with who matters more to him, Kingsfield or Kingsfield's daughter. Some choice: A person who's had enough of law students, or her father. For the daughter, Hart is willing to do nothing more than see her in private when it suits his schedule, but for the father, Hart will break into the law school library to steal Kingsfield's own class notes, taken when he was a Harvard student. For the love of promissory estoppel! Hart is smitten.

Near the film's end, there is a quick but revealing moment between Hart and Kingsfield as student approaches professor on an elevator they're sharing. The semester has ended and Hart summons the courage to declare his admiration for Kingsfield and his Contracts class. Kingsfield, who is only a monster in the minds of his those whose futures he will decide with the exams he is about to grade, looks beyond the perfect bow tie and at the student he's berated and complimented throughout the year—and asks him what his name is. This is quite a good film about the kill-or-be-killed pressures of law school and whether the paper is worth the chase. The classroom scenes are brutally authentic and may cause viewers who have not yet gone to law school to ask for a refund on their LSAT prep course.

Key Scene—The opening scene shows an empty, amphitheater classroom slowly filling with law students awaiting their inaugural class. Professor Kingsfield then enters the packed room and, without so much as a "Hello" or "Welcome to your worst nightmare," begins to discuss the case of *Hawkins v. McGee*, the contracts case I would imagine you know as "the hairy hand case," where a doctor's experimental skin graft on a boy's burnt hand resulted in a self-evidently titled lawsuit. Kingsfield calls out, "Mr. Hart!" and Hart quickly realizes to his shame that he should have been prepared for the first class. Contract damages are discussed in between the body blows Kingsfield lays on Hart.

Discussion Suggestion—Students in a Contracts class could first be assigned to look up *Hawkins v. McGee*, 84 N.H. 114, 146 A. 641 (N.H.1929) on Westlaw® or Lexis®, and after watching the scene, discuss if it comports with the court's decision or rationale. Students in any legal class could discuss the larger purpose of the scene: the quasi-tyranny at the onset of law school. Does the boot camp approach to the Socratic Method provide any benefit? If so, then why is it that by the second year of law school, students are rarely subjected to what Kingsfield dispenses so skillfully?

Key Scene—In another fantastic classroom scene, Professor Kingsfield pesters his students about the various excuses for nonperformance in a contract, but that do not result in breach, such as a material fact not being in existence. Later, the famous Carbolic Smoke Ball case (another law school favorite) is discussed as the students answer questions about the nature of consideration in a contract.

Discussion Suggestion—Finding the 1892 British case of *Carlill v Carbolic Smoke Ball Company* might be too much trouble for your students. But you could find it and then use it with the key scene to discuss consideration, and the unilateral versus bilateral contracts.

PHILADELPHIA (PG-13; 1993)

Key Themes: Wrongful termination, illegal discrimination, AIDS and the legal system
Best Classroom Use: Civil Procedure, Torts, Employment Law, Introduction to Paralegal
                        Studies

125 minutes   (strong language)
Cast: Tom Hanks, Denzel Washington, Jason Robards, Mary Steenburgen, Antonio
               Banderas

Considered to be one of the first mainstream films to deal directly with AIDS, *Philadelphia* is a touching story, if not a bit self-evident, that earned Tom Hanks his first Oscar. Hanks plays Andrew Beckett, a rising senior associate in a white-shoe Philadelphia law firm, where none of the partners know about his sexuality or his health, but all seem to know of his legal acumen. In fact, the senior and managing partner, Charles Wheeler (Jason Robards), gives Beckett the firm's newest and important corporate client. While celebrating with the other partners, one of them notices a sore on Becket's head, which Becket explains away as a racquetball injury. Even though he is suffering from a case of AIDS-related flu, Becket manages to get to the firm on the weekend to turn in the complaint for this important case. But, mysteriously, while recuperating at home, Becket is told that the complaint is missing and that there is no computer backup version either. After barely making the statute of limitations by redrafting the complaint, Becket is soon called into a partners' meeting, where he is dressed down by Wheeler—who tells him that he has an attitude and competency problem—and is then fired.

Believing he was fired because the partners learned that their star associate is gay with AIDS, Becket seeks representation for his wrongful termination claim. After nine law firms refuse his case—for reasons we can infer—Becket visits the cramped office of personal injury and TV advertising lawyer Joe Miller (Denzel Washington), whose race is but one of the many characteristics these two lawyers do not share. Miller isn't above slipping his business card to hospital patients and Salvation Army Christmas bell ringers, and doesn't want to be around homosexuals, much less near a sick one, but finally takes the case, perhaps hoping for the free publicity. *Philadelphia* is as much about Miller's personal journey as it is about Becket's legal claim and remaining time with his loved ones.

The legal facet of *Philadelphia* is straightforward: Becket and Miller try to establish that Wheeler and his partners wrongfully fired Becket in violation of civil rights and anti-discrimination law, while Wheeler and his legal team claim that Becket was fired for his incompetence and attitude. In fact, the partners claim that they couldn't have fired him for having AIDS because they didn't know, since Becket was so successful at hiding his sexuality and illness from them. This doesn't stop them from trying to smear Becket while making their defense, and using a female as lead counsel (Mary Steenburgen) to help bolster their nondiscriminatory stance. Miller's task is to unhinge the defendants on the witness stand without annoying the jury, some of whom might share the same prejudices against a man like Andrew Becket, as does Becket's former employer. While not a surprise from the film's beginning, the ending is still satisfying.

Key Scene—Denzel Washington's character, Joe Miller, witnesses his daughter's birth, but soon is soliciting patients in the hospital. He then meets with a prospective client whose claim about falling in a pothole seems a little forced. Miller takes the case and tells the new client that his secretary will discuss the fees arrangements. Andrew Becket then walks in, seeking Miller's representation. Miller's awkwardness towards Becket is palpable, and after Becket explains the circumstances of his firing and his wrongful termination theory, Miller says there is no case.

Discussion Suggestion—There is a lot to chew on in these connected scenes, starting with Miller's solicitation, and his lack of fees discussion with his new client. As to the heart of the scene, discuss what would need to be established in such a wrongful termination case, and whether there is any precedent that would prevent an employer from firing someone for having AIDS, assuming it could be proven. Also, discuss whether the law firm would be in a strong legal position to fire Becket without cause, if he was an at-will employee.

Key Scene—During a scene of the trial, Joe Miller examines a woman who worked at a firm where one of Wheeler's partners used to work. She announced to the firm that she had AIDS, and although she wasn't fired, she was treated like a pariah by that partner. On cross-examination, she testifies that she contracted HIV after a blood transfusion. Then, the lawyer says, "There was no behavior on your part that led to you contracting the virus; it was unavoidable." Miller doesn't object to that line of questioning or statement.

Discussion Suggestion—Should Miller have objected? If so, on what basis? Wouldn't questioning someone about "innocently" acquiring HIV be detrimental to a claim that you didn't discriminate against a homosexual who acquired HIV through unprotected sex?

Key Scene—The jury finds for Becket—who is too ill to attend the trial and is in the hospital—and awards him $243,000 in compensatory damages and $4,782 in punitive damages.

Discussion Suggestion—If you watched the entire film, discuss whether the evidence, as shown, established a wrongful termination. Although Becket's job performance seemed anything but incompetent, was it enough for Becket to show that his employer harbored stereotypical views about homosexuals, or told crude jokes about gays? Knowing Becket's cause of action, how was it proven? If there is time, you could research wrongful termination law, looking for a similar case or a statute that would fit the movie's premise.

PRESUMED INNOCENT (R; 1990)

Key Themes: Murder prosecution, litigation strategies, political maneuvering, revenge
Best Classroom Use: Criminal Law, Criminal Procedure, Evidence

127 minutes   (sexual situations, strong language)
Cast: Harrison Ford, Bonnie Bedelia, Greta Scacchi, Raul Julia, Paul Winfield

One of the best combinations of courtroom drama and character study, *Presumed Innocent,* from the superb Scott Turow novel, may be a little too sexual for classroom viewing. But, it is definitely worth recommending, and has key scenes that are worth watching. Harrison Ford, in one of his few nonheroic roles, plays Rusty Sabich, the chief deputy district attorney of a large Midwestern city. He is given the assignment of solving the brutal sexual murder of Carolyn Polhemus (Greta Scacchi), a woman with whom Rusty had been sleeping and obsessed, who also worked in his office as a calculating, junior assistant prosecutor.

Initially, Rusty is reticent to investigate the case, possibly because he—and his wife—realize the coincidence. But Rusty's boss and mentor is two weeks away from his reelection bid and desperately needs to make an arrest before his opponent, a former employee from the district attorney's office, uses the murder as campaign ammo. Rusty knows the phone calls he made to and from Carolyn's apartment will show up in the investigation, so he asks his chief investigator to officially ignore them, claiming the calls were work related. However, the further the investigation goes, more and more physical evidence points to Rusty. Eventually, he is charged with murdering Carolyn, and is thrown overboard by his friend and former boss.

Although she knows of her husband's past infidelity, Rusty's strangely loyal wife (Bonnie Bedelia) stands firmly beside him. Rusty seeks the help of superstar defense attorney Sandy Stern, played marvelously by Raul Julia. This plot thickens like a roux; everyone seems to have something to hide. At the time of her death, Carolyn was in possession of a secret, five-year-old public official bribery file investigating someone who is now more powerful but unknown. And, Rusty isn't the only one in city government who had been sleeping with the Carolyn, a woman whose beauty was exceeded by her cold ambition.

The trial scenes in *Presumed Innocent* are excellent, as the prosecution makes its case against the morbidly restrained defendant, trying to establish a sexual motive for the murder, even though it has no direct evidence that Rusty was sleeping with Carolyn. A key piece of physical evidence can't be found, and the autopsy and pathologist's notes don't add up. As the prosecution closes its case, Rusty and Sandy discuss whether Rusty will do more harm than good for his case by testifying in his own defense. And for those who have yet to see it, the ending is quite a shocker.

Key Scene—During a pretrial hearing, the judge rules on the prosecution's request to have its second chair prosecutor, Tommy Molto, testify about a conversation he had with Rusty in a hallway right after Rusty was told that a glass found at the scene of the murder had Rusty's fingerprints on it. After Molto had accused Rusty of murdering Carolyn, Rusty snapped back, "You're right. You're always right." Now, the newly elected district attorney wants Molto to testify about that conversation. The judge rules against the prosecution, finding that the statement is meaningless, and was nothing more than a retort by an angry man.

Discussion Suggestion—Upon viewing this scene, discuss how the admissibility of evidence is determined by weighing the evidence's probative and prejudicial value. Furthermore, discuss whether the hearsay rules would even allow for Molto's testimony on the hallway.

Key Scene—After Sandy Stern pounces all over the pathologist who had testified about the presence of diaphragm spermicide in the body of Carolyn—but missed that his autopsy notes show that Carolyn had her tubes tied—the state rests. This second huge gaffe in the prosecution's case seems to show that the pathologist logged the wrong bodily fluid sample as having come from the victim. Sandy then moves for a dismissal of the charges, and the judge grants the motion, telling the jury in a short speech that the prosecution failed to establish any direct evidence that Rusty murdered Carolyn, or even a motive for the murder. The judge, we've come to learn, was the one taking bribes years earlier to support his own affair with Carolyn, then apologizes in open court to Rusty for all he has been put through.

Discussion Suggestion—Is it required that a motive be proven in order for a guilty verdict to be rendered? If it isn't required, is it essential? And, is direct evidence exclusively needed to prove that someone committed murder? If you have watched the film rather than the key scenes, do you think the evidence presented was sufficient to convict Rusty Sabich?

PRIMAL FEAR (R; 1996)

Key Themes: Insanity defense, honesty in litigation, corruption in the Catholic Church and in government

Best Classroom Use: Criminal Law, Criminal Procedure, Legal Ethics

130 minutes   (nudity, sexual situation, violence, strong language)
Cast: Richard Gere, Edward Norton, Laura Linney, John Mahoney, Andre Braugher, Frances McDormand, Alfre Woodard

As envisioned, nothing is all that controversial about the insanity defense; if one fails to appreciate the wrongfulness of his or her conduct because of a mental illness or disease, then there is no criminal intent. As it has been applied since the delusional Daniel M'Naghten shot at the Prime Minister in 1841, killing his personal secretary instead, the insanity defense has been nothing if not controversial. *Primal Fear* uses this controversy to tell an interesting story about a lawyer's desire to promote himself in a murder case that involves the Catholic Church and a sex scandal, and just might include a government conspiracy.

The Chicago archbishop, beloved by everyone from the lowly to the powerful, is brutally sliced to death in his bedroom, and a mysterious call number is carved onto his chest. A young man is seen running from the scene covered in blood and is eventually captured. To the rescue comes Martin Vail (Richard Gere), Chicago's most famous and camera-loving defense lawyer. Martin visits the young Aaron Stampler (Edward Norton) in jail and offers to take the case *pro bono*. Prosecuting the case is an assistant district attorney (Laura Linney) who is Martin's ex-girlfriend, and who is being pressured by her boss's superior—a good friend of the archbishop—to get the death penalty. Although the evidence literally drips with Aaron's guilt, Martin believes Aaron's story that a third person was in the room with the archbishop, and that Aaron was passed out during the killing. Why a lawyer, who earlier tells a man in a bar that a good defense lawyer never even asks his client if he did it, would believe such an alibi makes little sense except in a movie. So, Martin's strategy is to dig deep into the archbishop's background to find who would have a motive for murdering him.

While Martin, his investigator, and paralegal proceed to dig up dirt on the dead priest, a psychiatrist hired by Martin begins digging at the mild-mannered, stammering Aaron Stampler, a young man who was literally rescued from the streets of Chicago by the archbishop, eventually becoming an altar boy. Martin and his team find possible murder suspects in the secret land deals the archbishop's charities have been investing in throughout the city—investments that have connections to halls of city and state government. The psychiatrist finds a possible murderer in Roy, the rough and violent alternate personality residing in Aaron, who takes ownership for the killing. But the juiciest discovery is the secret videotape in the archbishop's library, showing the archbishop himself filming and ordering Aaron to engage in sexual acts with another young man and a girl. Hello motive.

As Martin tries to decide what to do with the videotape, he realizes his client was telling the truth…sort of. If Roy committed the murder, then Aaron isn't guilty of it. But since Martin believes he won't be allowed to change Aaron's plea during the trial from "not guilty" to "not guilty by reason of insanity," Martin devises quite a strategy to get Aaron's insanity—and Roy's testimony—injected into the trial. Martin's risky tactic works to perfection, but the film's final scenes show just how sick Aaron really is.

Key Scene—Martin Vail heads to the archbishop's home in search of the explosive videotape. Upon finding it, he switches it with another videotape he brought with him. Watching the video back in his office, Martin realizes the extent of Aaron's/Roy's motive for murder, but believes he can't change his client's plea during the middle of the trial. Since Martin has stolen the video, he knows he can't disclose it at the trial, so he orders his investigator to drop a copy off at the prosecutor's home, and make her responsible for its contents. When her boss (and close friend of the archbishop) becomes aware of the tape, he orders her to destroy the copy.

Discussion Suggestion—You could have a field day discussing which lawyers committed what ethics violations during these vignettes. Beyond that, analyze what, if anything, Martin Vail could have done upon realizing there is a video implicating the archbishop in sexcapades with the defendant.

Key Scene—Facing a career-killing quandary, the prosecutor attempts to get the videotape into evidence by first calling Martin Vail's private investigator as a witness. Martin immediately objects, arguing that his investigator is covered by the work product rule, but the judge overrules him, and the investigator is questioned about his connection to the video.

Discussion Suggestion—Upon watching this scene, discuss whether the work product rule even applies in this situation. The attorney-client privilege might cover the investigator's possible testimony more aptly than the work product rule, but you could examine your own jurisdiction's rules of evidence to see how either would apply to the nonlawyer employee of a client's lawyer.

Key Scene—The final scene shows how depraved Aaron Stampler really is. His split personality was not only a drop-dead-accurate ruse, but there really was no "Aaron" all along. Martin Vail leaves the courthouse with the mega-chagrin of knowing that he has just unwittingly helped a sociopath get away with murder.

Discussion Suggestion—Is there anything Martin can legally or ethically do?

THE RAINMAKER (PG-13; 1997)

Key Themes: Insurance company and wrongful death litigation, David versus Goliath,
                      lawyer ethics violations
Best Classroom Use: Legal Ethics, Civil Procedure, Litigation, Introduction to Paralegal Studies

135 minutes   (strong language, violence)
Cast: Matt Damon, Danny DeVito, John Voight, Danny Glover, Claire Danes, Mary
               Kay Place, Mickey Rourke, Teresa Wright, Virginia Madsen

Nearly perfect for a classroom setting, *The Rainmaker* is rich with professional responsibility
quandaries. Unlikely as it may be that a brand new lawyer could take on an insurance company,
backed by a high-powered legal team, there is much to be gained by watching this film, originally
a John Grisham novel.

Fresh and broke from law school, former idealist Rudy Baylor (Matt Damon) can't avoid
working for a personal injury lawyer named Bruiser (Mickey Rourke), whose office is in a strip
mall and whose cases are scrounged up by the self-proclaimed "paralawyer" Deck Shiffler
(Danny DeVito), who has flunked the bar six times. Bruiser's arrangement with Rudy is that
Rudy must pay his own way by bringing cases to Bruiser, who will give Rudy a cut of the fees.
Fortunately, Rudy has brought a few cases with him. He is working on a will for on old widow
who claims to be worth millions, and has the case of a poor family whose son is dying of
leukemia and was denied repeated requests for medical treatment coverage by Great Benefits
Insurance Company. While representing these clients and studying for the bar exam, Rudy is sent
with paralawyer Deck Shiffler to fish for clients at a Memphis hospital. They catch wind of
Bruiser's impending federal indictment, so before they are roped into the mess, they decide to
split with their case files and start their own little firm. In the meantime, Rudy rents an apartment
from the not-so-rich widow for whom he has written a will, and falls in love with a young,
abused married girl (Claire Danes) who eventually becomes his client.

Rudy is facing a Herculean task as he and Deck—one who has never represented a client in court
and one who has no right to do so—try to prepare their case against the obviously greedy insurance
company, defended by the loathsome Leo Drummond (John Voight), whose patronization of Rudy
is the most honest thing he does. The dirty tricks Leo's team use range from colluding with the
first judge on the case to have Rudy believe the case should settle for a low amount, to having
witnesses disappear just before scheduled depositions, to bugging Rudy's office. Rudy and Deck,
however, are not as pure as the wind-driven snow, and use some of their own tricks to try to even
the playing field. The second judge (Danny Glover) senses what Rudy is up against, and gives the
new lawyer as much leeway as is reasonable. Proving that Great Benefits wrongfully denied
Donny Ray Black's claim as a matter of business practice is difficult, since the key witness and
internal documents are missing. But thanks to Deck's chicanery and unique legal research, Rudy
gives to Mrs. Black the victory she desires.

Key Scene—Rudy Baylor visits Miss Birdie, the widow in need of a will. She believes she is worth millions of dollars, and would like to leave none of it to her adult children. "Cut, cut, cut," she says, in reference to them. Instead, she wants to leave her putative estate to her favorite televangelist, who she says needs a new jet. After cautioning Miss Birdie about her wishes, Rudy begins to leave, and notices an apartment above her garage. Being in need of a new place to live, he asks to rent her apartment, suggesting he could also help with her yard work. Miss Birdie now is his client and landlord.

Discussion Suggestion—Can someone disinherit their children? If so, how? Is there any problem with Rudy becoming a tenant of his client? The ethics rules in some jurisdictions have warnings about lawyers and clients having business relationships.

Key Scene—In one of the funnier scenes from the film, Deck Shiffler takes Rudy to the hospital in search of new clients. Rudy objects to this, but Deck tells Rudy that Rudy didn't learn the right things in law school about being a lawyer, as Deck easily skirts past the front desk and finds his way into a patient room. There, a man lies in traction. In a matter of about a minute, Deck, calling himself a "paralawyer," signs up this prospective client, even helping the poor guy sign the retainer agreement, while Deck says, "We're going to get you a bunch of money." Out the door Deck and Rudy go, with Rudy shocked at what just happened.

Discussion Suggestion—Use your jurisdiction's ethics rules to analyze and discuss the amazing solicitation that has just taken place. Also, did you take note of Deck's "paralawyer" title? Discuss who would be responsible for Deck's illegal solicitation.

Key Scene—Bruiser takes Rudy and Deck to lunch to celebrate Rudy's passing of the bar exam. After Bruiser leaves, Deck and Rudy discuss their future, considering the papers are reporting that Bruiser is under federal investigation and is about to be indicted. Deck tells Rudy that they should get their case files—including the Great Benefits file—from Bruiser's office before the feds shut the office down, and then start their own firm, splitting everything 50/50. After a little contemplation, Rudy agrees, and the two of them set up shop in a dilapidated office building.

Discussion Suggestion—Can a lawyer and nonlawyer split fees with each other, much less be in partnership together? What source of law speaks to this?

Key Scene—After they realize their office has been bugged, Deck and Rudy set up a sting operation making fake phone calls to ensnare Leo Drummond, who they believe is behind the bugging. Then, Deck and Rudy get their least favorite prospective juror kicked off the panel by making Drummond think that Rudy and the man have talked on the phone, with the man expressing his sympathy for the plaintiffs' plight. After an in-court scuffle with the actual prospective juror, Drummond realizes that Rudy and Deck were one step ahead of his duplicity.

Discussion Suggestion—Does Rudy have a duty to report Drummond's bugging to the judge? Although the shrewd strategy works like a charm, isn't Rudy being dishonest too?

Key Scene—After using subterfuge to find Jackie Lamancyzk (Virginia Madsen), a former claims examiner from Great Benefits who holds the key to the lawsuit, Deck takes her to Rudy, and he takes her to court. Along with her testimony, she presents a claims manual that has the secret Section U, which instructs claims employees to reject all medical claims. The defense argues that this evidence cannot be admitted because it was stolen from the company by Jackie, and the judge temporarily agrees. Doing some quick work, Deck finds Bruiser, who helps Deck find a case on point, holding that stolen evidence can be admitted if the lawyer desiring to have the evidence admitted was not involved with the theft. When presented with this case the next day, the judge changes his ruling and admits Jackie's employee claims manual into evidence.

Discussion Suggestion—Conduct your own research to see if there is any precedent on whether evidence reputed to have been stolen can be admitted.

RUNAWAY JURY (PG-13; 2003)

Key Themes: Honesty in litigation, jury tampering, situational ethics
Best Classroom Use: Civil Procedure, Legal Ethics, Introduction to Paralegal Studies

127 minutes   (violence, strong language)
Cast: John Cusack, Gene Hackman, Dustin Hoffman, Rachel Weisz

Groucho Marx once said he would never belong to a club that would have him as a member. Today, he might say he wouldn't want to be on a jury that consisted of others like himself, incapable of avoiding jury duty. From a long list of John Grisham novels turned into movies comes this film. But where the source material centered on a big tobacco lawsuit, the film version of *Runaway Jury* makes gun manufacturers the bad guys. When a stockbroker is murdered by a former day trader gone on a rampage at the brokerage firm, the broker's widow sues the gun manufacturer, alleging it is liable for negligently making such assault-type weapons so readily available without any compunction of its consequences.

One would expect the stakes to be skyscraper high for such a groundbreaking case, and so it is not much of a surprise that the defense would use the services of a jury consultant. And to have the infamous consultant Rankin Finch (Gene Hackman) on your side means that you can almost guarantee a victory, considering he and his crack staff employ the technology and tactics that would have driven the Watergate plumbers insanely jealous. Not only does the defendant, Vicksburg Arms, believe it will have the jury on its side, it and a few other gun manufacturers have conspired to pay a fee into the tens of millions of dollars, if needed, to ensure the outcome. The plaintiff's attorney, Wendell Rohr (Dustin Hoffman), has his own jury consultant, sort of, but not someone with the ammo of Rankin Finch. However, being outgunned doesn't bother attorney Rohr, because he believes he has justice on his side.

As the prospective jurors are being analyzed in court and in secret, Nick Easter (John Cusack) sits impatiently in the gallery, waiting his turn. Two things just aren't right about Easter—Rankin didn't know he was in the jury pool, and Easter seems coolly uninterested in being on the jury. Easter becomes Juror No. 9 on the biggest public policy case in decades, and sets about subtly influencing the other jurors before the opening statements begin. Then, a mysterious woman (Rachel Weisz) sends a message to Rankin that she can guarantee a defense verdict for $10 million. The woman, who is Easter's girlfriend, then makes the same extortion to Wendell Rohr. So, as Rankin strives to uncover and deal with the scheming juror, Rohr decides while trying the case whether or not he is going to chuck his ethics (too late) and pay a bribe. The mystery woman plays both ends against the middle, and Easter continues to work on the jurors, finding the right alliance to get the verdict he will need.

The mystery of the movie isn't just whether the jury will vote for the widow or the gun manufacturer, but also who Nick Easter is and what is motivating him. Although the conclusion is wrapped too neatly and the implication is that the ends justify the means, *Runaway Jury* does raise important issues about the intrusion of jury consulting into the system of justice, and whether it is right to render a verdict because the cause it represents is greater than the evidence would allow.

Key Scene—Marlee, Nick Easter's girlfriend, meets with the great Wendell Rohr to discuss the $10 million extortion offer she previously made to him. He is, of course, indignant at the outset, but she actually begins to convince him that buying the jury isn't so much a breach of all legal ethics and propriety, but is actually a fundamental step towards getting the gun laws changed and making the gun manufacturers pay for all their transgressions. After the plaintiff's key witness, a former executive of Vicksburg Arms, fails to appear (as was predicted), Wendell Rohr and Rankin Finch have a heated exchange over the meaning of justice and the value of the jury system. Then, Rohr goes to his firm's key partners to ask for the needed millions to buy his "just verdict."

Discussion Suggestion—Discuss the present relevance of the jury system in America, whether it still serves the ideals for which it was originally intended. If there were no more juries, and only judges were fact finders, it would seem that the jury consulting industry would have to fold. Also, discuss your opinions on Wendell Rohr's own morality and ethics. It is easy to see how the movie portrays the defense lawyers and consultants as corrupt, but Rohr's actions in these scenes show him also to lack integrity.

THE STAR CHAMBER (R; 1983)

Key Themes: Justice versus law, legal technicalities, misuse of power
Best Classroom Use: Criminal Procedure, Legal Ethics

109 minutes   (violence, profanity)
Cast: Michael Douglas, Hal Holbrook, Yaphet Kotto, James B. Sikking, Sharon Gless

Beginning in 1487 and for about 150 years, a not-so-secret court called The Star Chamber met at the Royal Palace of Westminster. Distinct from other courts, the Star Chamber was initially well regarded as an efficient judicial forum. Eventually, its misuse of power led to its dismissal. In today's parlance, "star chamber" refers to any tribunal that renders its decisions (and enforcements) in secret and without procedural safeguards. Borrowing loosely from the historical legend, this hard-to-find film is a worthy morality tale on the tension between justice and legal technicalities. Unfortunately, *The Star Chamber* turns into a thriller.

As if made for a critic of the Warren Court's decisions in search and seizure cases, this movie is set in Los Angeles—Earl Warren's city of birth—as news reports spill the details of the heinous murders of elderly women. After the police capture the suspect red-handed, the defendant's lawyer gets all the evidence, and then the charges, thrown out on what seems to be a minor technicality. Although told by the prosecutor that this decision will release a serial murder, Judge Hardin (Michael Douglas) believes the law requires such a result. Later, when two suspected child rapists and murderers are arrested and find themselves in Judge Hardin's court, he once again, but not without soul searching, rules against the prosecution, throwing out the evidence of the crime found in the defendant's van. The dead boy's grief-stricken father then takes the law into his own hands, and finds himself in jail. "What happened to right and wrong?" Judge Hardin asks his wife as he contemplates his role in freeing the defendants.

Judge Hardin's mentor and fellow judge (Hal Holbrook) has an answer, and sensing Judge Hardin's desperation, the seasoned judge says to his mentor, "Someone has kidnapped justice and hidden it in the law." Hal Holbrook then invites the younger judge to join a cadre of other judges who meet in secret to decide the fates of prior defendants whose obvious guilt was protected by legal technicalities. After hearing a summary of the dismissed cases, the judges vote and send a hit man to carry out the sentences. As preposterous as that seems, authenticity is strived for more successfully here than in *The Life of David Gale*, another agenda-film, since excellent police work shows that the two child murderer suspects released by Judge Hardin's procedural decisions were, in fact, innocent, and the star chamber was wrong when it voted to have the men killed for their crimes. Now, Judge Hardin is faced with quite a dilemma: do nothing and chalk up that mistake as the cost of doing business, or do something and risk exposing himself and the others as conspirators and murderers.

Key Scene—Undercover police suspect something is awry when watching a man walking through a bad part of Los Angeles early in the morning. Their hunch is correct and as the chase ensues, the suspect drops a revolver in his trash can before entering his house. The officers believe they need a warrant to search the trash can, since it and its contents are the property of the suspect (who turns out to be the serial murderer of the elderly women). They then decide that once the trash can is dumped into the garbage truck, a search warrant will no longer be necessary. So, they wait a few minutes before recovering the gun from the garbage truck's well. But their tactics are challenged by a crafty defense lawyer who argues that there was still a reasonable expectation of privacy in the defendant's garbage, since when the revolver was recovered, that garbage had yet to mix with other garbage in the truck. Judge Hardin reluctantly agrees, and the evidence and the case against the murderer are tossed.

Discussion Suggestion—Discuss the credulity of such a scene, particularly in light of the plain view, and exigent circumstances exceptions to search warrant law. One might consider taking that fact pattern and having a memorandum of law drafted on the admissibility of the seized revolver.

Key Scene—In a reminiscent scene, two police officers pull over a van with some wild-eyed drug users inside who were looking for a liquor store to rob. Realizing there are outstanding warrants on the van for unpaid tickets, one of the officers feigns a smell of marijuana coming from inside, which leads to a warrantless search and the discovery of the bloody sneaker of a murdered boy. But it is to no avail since Judge Hardin rules in favor of the defendants at the evidentiary hearing, excluding the evidence on the grounds that the search was illegal because it was predicated on the outstanding warrants, which were defective due to a clerical error. The case is dismissed and the defendants are released.

Discussion Suggestion—Would a clerical error in a warrant render seized evidence inadmissible?

SUSPECT (R; 1987)

Key Themes: Murder trial, prosecution of the helpless, juror misconduct, lawyer misconduct, judicial misconduct
Best Classroom Use: Criminal Law, Criminal Procedure, Legal Ethics, Interviewing

120 minutes   (violence, strong language)
Cast: Cher, Dennis Quaid, Liam Neeson, John Mahoney, Joe Mantegna

If you're thinking that an R-rated legal movie starring Cher as a criminal defense attorney representing accused murderer Liam Neeson will require that she sleeps with her client, you're wrong. Cher sleeps with a juror instead, but only after the case is over. And that may be the least ethically-challenged activity she does with the juror throughout the trial. In defense to Cher, the juror is Dennis Quaid, and he did do some amazing amateur detective work to help her prove who the real murderer is, so all's well that ends well.

Cher stars as Kathleen Riley, a Washington D.C. public defender who, naturally, is overworked and underpaid. So lousy is her life that on her way to work, she gets attacked in her car and has Christmas presents stolen from her back seat by the very people who, if arrested, would be her clients, notwithstanding the interest conflict. At least she's alive, which is more than can be said about the two people who open the film. A young woman, who we later learn was a clerk typist at the Justice Department, meets a Supreme Court Justice at his chambers and he gives her an envelope and then thanks her. Upon her exit, the Justice pulls out a shotgun from its leather case and puts it in his mouth. Bang. Then, the young woman is found dead in a D.C. river near where her car was parked in a parking garage, with her neck sliced open. Tens of homeless people live nearby and one of them (Liam Neeson) is found with a bloody knife and her purse. At his first court appearance, the catatonic and disheveled defendant is given to Ms. Riley, who needs another client like a Supreme Court Justice needs a hole in the head.

The homeless man's name is Carl Wayne Anderson, and what no one initially realizes about him is that he can neither hear nor speak. While the case against him seems open and shut, Kathleen Riley bonds with this forgotten and forsaken Vietnam veteran, whose deafness and muteness are the result of a V.A. hospital infection. So onward she presses, even though she has little chance of success in a courtroom run by a harsh and brittle trial judge (John Mahoney), who has asked a colleague for this trial and is awaiting his nomination to the D.C. Circuit Court of Appeals.

It wouldn't be easy for any public defender to find a jury that won't prejudge a homeless man who was found within feet of the victim's body in possession of her purse and a bloody knife. Thank goodness that Eddie Sanger (Dennis Quaid), a Washington lobbyist with a keen eye for detail, makes it through *voir dire*. From the outset, he thinks there is more to the story than what the prosecutor (Joe Mantegna) is selling and what Ms. Riley realizes. In the spirit of The Hardy Boys, Sanger begins to investigate the case from inside and outside the jury box. Considering he's a dairy lobbyist who is willing to sleep with a member of Congress just to get a vote on a piece of milk legislation postponed, Sanger doesn't wrestle with the propriety of breaking through the fourth wall of the jury system. He begins by giving semi-anonymous tips to Ms. Riley, and eventually, Sanger and Riley are hunting down possible suspects and breaking into Justice

Department offices late in the evening. Riley initially tries to resist Sanger's illegal efforts and romantic overtures, but she assuages her guilt by focusing on the good she's trying to accomplish. She's made for the nation's capitol.

As the conspiracy begins taking shape and the connection between the Supreme Court Justice's suicide, his unethical activities decades earlier, and the woman's murder is drawing closer, the soon-to-be-promoted trial judge ratchets up his unforgiving approach to Kathleen Riley's pleas for a continuance and other evidentiary allowances. Not to give away the ending, but just imagine the foreshadowing the film's director implies by making this judge a Republican. While Cher is not exactly Gregory Peck and *Suspect* is not quite *To Kill a Mockingbird*, the film entertains nonetheless and provides a few key scenes worthy of consideration.

Key Scene—After being appointed to represent Carl Wayne Anderson, a dirty and smelly homeless man, Kathleen Riley interviews him, or at least tries to. Carl has nothing to say and attacks her as she leaves his jail cell. Back at her apartment, Riley is struck to realize that her new client is deaf. She goes back to see Carl and this time he's tied down to a gurney. Their interview takes place courtesy of a legal pad and pen.

Discussion Suggestion—Students in an Interviewing class could discuss what techniques need to be employed to interview clients with special needs. Did Cher do anything in her interview that is either to be recommended or avoided?

Key Scene—During the scene where Dennis Quaid's character is picked for jury duty, the prosecutor and Kathleen Riley question prospective jurors. One juror is dismissed by the defense because he, a loan officer, expresses no compunction about foreclosing on people who don't pay their mortgages. Eddie Sanger makes it through the *voir dire*, after being asked by the prosecutor about his views on crime and then asked by Kathleen about his lobbying background, and their exchange becomes prickly.

Discussion Suggestion—Can lawyers ask prospective jurors the questions that are shown in this scene? Perhaps you could discuss your experiences as an attorney.

Key Scene—Eddie Sanger makes another "anonymous" phone call to Kathleen Riley late one night, telling her to meet him at a certain public place. At that meeting, Eddie discusses a presidential cuff link he found at the scene of the crime, which he believes portends a Washington conspiracy. Also at the secret gathering is the mysterious and deadly homeless man named Michael, the one Carl Wayne Anderson said was at the crime scene before him. Michael nearly kills Kathleen and cuts Eddie with a switchblade. Kathleen administers first aid to Eddie back in her office, where he tries to kiss her.

Discussion Suggestion—This isn't that taxing an endeavor, but you could show the scene in Legal Ethics and then give a pop quiz, asking your students to estimate what ethics rules or criminal laws were broken, notwithstanding the attempted murder. They could conduct a bit of research to see if there are any disciplinary cases in their jurisdiction involving a lawyer (or judge) who was involved with a juror during a pending case.

Key Scene—Carl Wayne Anderson testifies in his own defense, using an electric writing pad. During the cross-examination, the prosecutor berates Carl about his history of violence and whether he had attacked his own attorney Kathleen. She quickly objects on the grounds that such an event, if it occurred, was privileged, and the prosecutor withdraws the question.

Discussion Suggestion—Does any privilege (attorney-client or even work product) protect Carl from having to answer that question? Remind your students what the attorney-client privilege (most likely found in your jurisdiction's witness competency statute) is and how it is different from the ethics rule on client confidentiality.

Key Scene—Late in the film, Kathleen breaks into the murder victim's car, still in the same parking lot as the night the woman was murdered, and finds in the cassette deck a tape recording made by the suicidal Supreme Court Justice. On it, he confesses his role in a decades-long bribe he was part of, which is the key to the murder mystery. Kathleen then unwittingly goes to the trial judge's home that very night, where he is having a dinner party attended by the deputy attorney general. She begins by telling the judge that she needs a continuance because of newly discovered evidence. When she sees the deputy attorney general she becomes frightened and apologizes to the judge for bothering him and leaves.

Discussion Suggestion—Although the purpose of this scene is to throw off the viewer about who the real killer is, sharp students in an Ethics class might notice that this is *ex parte* communication and there doesn't seem to be any exigency that would justify it.

A Time to Kill (R; 1996)

Key Themes: Racism and legal prejudice, vigilantism and the insanity defense, jury nullification and justice

Best Classroom Use: Criminal Law, Criminal Procedure, Introduction to Paralegal Studies, Legal Ethics

150 minutes (brutal rape scene and other graphic violence, strong language)
Cast: Matthew McConaughey, Samuel L. Jackson, Sandra Bullock, Kevin Spacey, Donald Sutherland

A Time to Kill is a straightforward legal drama about racism and justice in a small Mississippi town. It has all the traditional characters of a John Grisham book: The idealistic and inexperienced lawyer, the trusty assistant, the politically carnivorous and ethically challenged opposing lawyer, the crooked judge, and the sympathetic client who is a poor outsider up against a legal system not made for him. One of the more difficult movies on this list to watch, this story has many subplots and astonishingly horrible acts, including a child rape and attempted murder, courthouse killings, Ku Klux Klan attacks, police abuses, a race riot, a fire bombing, a sniper attack, a bomb planting, a house burning, a kidnapping, and more.

Two racist rednecks brutally rape a small black girl in Canton, Mississippi, leaving her for dead. They are arrested by the sheriff and await an arraignment in jail. The girl's father, Carl Lee Haley (Samuel L. Jackson), is beset with grief and a belief shaped by his life as a poor black man in the deep south that his daughter will not get justice. So, he takes justice into his own hands and shoots and kills the two rapists in the courthouse, and then goes home to await his arrest. Having been charged with two counts of first-degree murder by a pompous district attorney (Kevin Spacey) with his eye on much higher office, Carl Lee turns to Jake Brigance (Matthew McConaughey), who already feels guilty at having done nothing when Carl Lee implied his intentions to Jake before the shooting. Rather than seeking a plea bargain for voluntary manslaughter (a killing occurring during the sudden heat of a legitimate provocation), Carl Lee pleads not guilty by reason of insanity.

Jake is almost alone in this legal fight, and nearly loses his penniless client to the NAACP's legal defense team, who hopes to use Carl Lee's case for fundraising purposes. But Jake has a mentor (Donald Sutherland), a disbarred and often drunk former lawyer, and he also has Ellen Roark (Sandra Bullock), an eager law student and vehement death penalty opponent who comes to town, volunteering her time to help mount this most curious and statistically ineffective defense. The district attorney is a blustering political animal seeking the death penalty who is not above jury tampering. Despite the deep racial divisions in this community, the trial judge refuses to grant a change of venue, which means that Jake must try to convince a white and likely prejudiced jury that his client deserves a not guilty verdict. As the case moves forward, the KKK tries to scare and then kill off Jake, his family, and associates. At trial, both sides' experts testify whether Carl Lee knew right from wrong when he killed the two officially-alleged rapists. Then Carl Lee takes the stand and leaves no doubt about his state of mind. Facing defeat, Jake presents a closing argument that is short on the facts, but long on pathos. Considering the source material, the film's conclusion is no surprise.

Key Scene—After the rapists are arrested, Carl Lee stops by Jake's office. They know each other casually, and Carl Lee implies to Jake, who has his own young daughter, that Carl Lee will take the law into his own hands, even asking for Jake's legal help, if need be. Later that night, Jake tells his wife about the conversation, and she urges him to go to the sheriff. Following Carl Lee's courthouse slayings, Jake is wracked with guilt over his inaction.

Discussion Suggestion—This is an interesting confidentiality scene to discuss, since it isn't clear whether Carl Lee qualifies as Jake's prospective client before the killings. If Carl Lee's visit doesn't qualify as actually seeking legal assistance in its traditional sense, then Jake owes Carl Lee no duty of confidentiality. If it does, then Jake would have the privilege of breaching client confidentiality. Supposing Carl Lee had talked to a paralegal, would he or she have the same privilege? Use your jurisdiction's ethics rules to discuss this scene.

Key Scene—District attorney Rufus Buckley discusses with his staff the likelihood that Jake Brigance will file a motion for change of venue. Buckley will oppose the motion because, as he explains, their county has a 30 percent black population, which is much lower than any other surrounding county. Keeping Carl Lee's case at home will help ensure a much whiter, pro-death penalty jury pool. Although Buckley doesn't make this his official argument, he does win the motion, thanks to a crooked trial judge.

Discussion Suggestion—When is a change of venue due to pretrial publicity warranted? Would Carl Lee be entitled to a trial in a different county with a higher black population, for the sake of fairness?

Key Scene—The state calls its insanity expert to the stand and he testifies about the M'Naghten insanity standard, and concludes, based on his investigation, that Carl Lee was not insane when he shot and killed the two men who raped his daughter. Jake cross-examines the expert, and thanks to Ellen's burglary of the psychiatrist's office, gets him to acknowledge that he always testifies for the state and almost never concludes a defendant was insane, and that residing in his own hospital is a criminally insane man who the psychiatrist had testified was sane, but who the jury found was not.

Discussion Suggestion—This is a good scene for a discussion on the M'Naghten test, and the other insanity standards, such as the irresistible impulse test, the Durham standard, and the Model Penal Code's substantial capacity standard. Apply your jurisdiction's insanity statute to Carl Lee's case and discuss whether Carl Lee meets that standard, which would be highly unlikely.

Key Scene—The defense's insanity expert testifies that Carl Lee experienced a dissociative condition and was unaware of the consequences of his actions, and couldn't tell right from wrong. Buckley's cross-examination focuses on an unknown felony the expert had pleaded guilty to in 1960. Upon stating he never had a felony, the psychiatrist is trapped in a lie, as Buckley shows the records and news clippings proving that the psychiatrist committed statutory rape. After this meltdown, Jake doesn't rehabilitate his witness.

Discussion Suggestion—If you have seen both psychiatrist scenes, you could discuss whose view of Carl Lee's mental state on that fateful day is more plausible, bearing in mind that the movie presents the M'Naghten standard as applicable in Mississippi. Was Carl Lee really insane? Doesn't his case seem like one better suited for voluntary manslaughter?

Key Scene—The closing arguments by both sides are moving, with Buckley appealing to the jury's sense of ordered justice, and Jake begging the jury to think on the horrific facts of the rape and attempted murder of Carl Lee's daughter, and to pretend that she was white. Carl Lee is found not guilty.

Discussion Suggestion—The biggest question of all from this movie is whether the verdict was legally correct, in light of the evidence.

THANK YOU FOR SMOKING (R; 2005)

Key Themes: Smoking and the law, deceit and cover-up, lobbying and government
Best Classroom Use: Torts, Business Law, Ethics

91 minutes   (strong language, sexual situations)
Cast: Aaron Eckhart, Katie Holmes, Robert Duvall, William H. Macy, Rob Lowe,
             Sam Elliott

Before Christopher Buckley was disinherited in 2008 by the modern conservative movement and *National Review*, the magazine founded by his late father, William F. Buckley, Jr., for publicly supporting Barak Obama's campaign, Buckley was more famous for his satire than his politics. Based on the younger Buckley's novel, *Thank You for Smoking* doesn't deny that smoking is deadly and that the lobbyists who push it are brazen, but it asks the viewer to consider if the political class and do-gooders who are trying to stomp it out might be equally unhealthy.

Nick Naylor (Aaron Eckhart) has what may be the worst job in the country: He asks us to smoke cigarettes and makes no apologies for it. He is best summed up by the last line in the film, a self-referential bon mot, "Michael Jordan plays ball, Charles Manson kills people, I talk. Everyone has a talent." Boy, does he ever. While sitting on the stage of the Joan Lunden show, next to a teenage cancer survivor and former smoker, and while being booed by the studio audience, Naylor defends the tobacco industry by saying that it would never want smokers to die because it would lose its customers. He then promises a $50 million, teen, antismoking advertising campaign (which wasn't approved by his employer, the ironically titled Academy of Tobacco Sciences), and shakes the hand of the ashen and bald teen, to the delight and cheers of the audience.

Naylor's boss at the Academy of Tobacco Sciences is none too thrilled about the $50 million pledge, but more concerned about Vermont Senator Ortolan Finistirre (Willam H. Macey), who is leading his own campaign to have a huge skull and crossbones placed on the front of every cigarette pack in America, a precursor to criminalizing tobacco. At an office meeting where the topic is how to improve the public's perception of smoking and rescue dwindling market share, Naylor suggests that smoking be re-incorporated into the consciousness of moviegoers, as was the case during the 1930s where smoking onscreen was pervasive. So why not go back to the good old days, but this time pay off the movie studios to have their biggest stars lighting up onscreen. Soon, Naylor is summoned to Winston-Salem, North Carolina, to meet with the Captain (Robert Duvall), big tobacco's founding father, and the plan is given a go-ahead.

Meanwhile, Naylor is going to be the subject of a major newspaper piece written by Washington investigative journalist Heather Holloway (Katie Holmes). Naylor's two lobbyist friends—one who works for the alcohol industry, and the other for the gun industry—warn him about the Delilah-like charms of the beautiful reporter, but to no avail. As soon as the clothing comes off, Sampson spills the beans. Off to Hollywood Naylor goes, with his 10-year-old son in tow, to strike a deal with a Hollywood studio head (Rob Lowe). For $25 million, Naylor can secure that Brad Pitt and Catherine Zeta Jones will light up after what is often done before lighting up cigarettes.

Naylor actually garners some sympathy in the press after he is kidnapped by antismoking terrorists who almost make good on their public promise to kill him. But the good press wanes when Ms. Holloway's above-the-fold article appears in the newspaper, exposing all the secrets Naylor divulged to her in what he stupidly thought was off the record pillow talk. Not appreciating that their number one mouthpiece has told a reporter about the Hollywood payoff and other dirty deeds, like secret payments to the cancer-ridden and dying Marlboro Man, Nick's employer fires him.

With the encouragement of his son, of all people, Naylor stages a comeback from disgrace by turning the tables on Ms. Holloway and keeping his date to testify before Senator Finistirre's antismoking hearings. Naylor has previously eviscerated the senator from the cheddar cheese state on national TV, but what he has in store here conjures the boldness of Ollie North and the Iran-Contra hearings. Although this film isn't technically a legal film, its use of satire to examine one of the country's biggest public policy issues makes it readily adaptable to legal courses.

Key Scene—Nick Naylor and his son are in Los Angeles, where Nick is scheduled to meet with a Hollywood executive about inserting more cigarettes into key movie scenes. At the meeting, the movie mogul discusses what kinds of movies would be amenable for smoking, and what it would cost. Then at the Santa Monica Pier, Nick and his son discuss lobbying and the art of arguing over ice cream flavors. It's a short discussion but enlightening. Later in the evening, the mogul calls Naylor to tell him that he can get Brad Pitt and Catherine Zeta Jones to smoke in a love scene for $25 million and co-financing of the picture.

Discussion Suggestion—Have Naylor and the movie mogul committed conspiracy? Has Naylor committed the crime of bribery? Are these crimes or just sharp business practices?

Key Scene—After being fired, Naylor still testifies before Senator Finistirre's subcommittee. The senator from Vermont thinks he's prepared for Naylor's tricks, having learned his lesson from being gut shot by Naylor on The Dennis Miller Show a few weeks earlier. But when questioned about the evils of smoking, Naylor not only doesn't deny the obvious, he uses the danger of cigarettes as a springboard into the dangers associated in the native states of the other senators (cars in Michigan, for instance), and tackles Senator Finistirre about the evils of his beloved Vermont: cholesterol-laden, artery-clogging cheddar cheese. Let him without sin cast the first stone.

Discussion Suggestion—This scene encapsulates all that passes for argument on both sides of the cigarette debate. On a broader note, students can discuss whether the auto industry and the cheese industry, or any producer of meat, sun tan lotion, breast implants, butter and other dairy products, not to mention junk food, should be civilly liable for the negative effects associated with their products. How much of a role should law or government have when it comes to matters of what some call unhealthy appetites?

TO KILL A MOCKINGBIRD (NR; 1962)

Key Themes: Social injustice, racism, rape trial
Best Classroom Use: Introduction to Law, Criminal Law

130 minutes   (violence, strong language)
Cast: Gregory Peck, Mary Badham, Phillip Alford, John Megna, Brock Peters, Robert Duvall

To state the obvious, this is a thoroughly rewarding film to watch, and is much more than a courtroom drama. It is also the only film on this list to be part of the American Film Institute's 100 Greatest American Movies (at number 34). Gregory Peck won an Academy Award for playing Atticus Finch, a southern lawyer in a depression-era small town, who represents a black man accused of raping and beating a white woman. More important than being an attorney, Atticus is also a parent, a widower raising two precocious children who call their father by his first name.

The movie's protagonist is Scout (Mary Badham), Atticus's six-year-old tomboy of a daughter, who personifies Harper Lee, the Pulitzer Prize winning author of *To Kill a Mockingbird,* and whose attorney-father was the inspiration for Atticus Finch. The movie is much like a three-act play, with the first and third acts involving childhood curiosity and exploration into the mystery of Boo Radley (Robert Duvall, in his first movie role), the rarely seen young man living with his parents down the street, whose slow mental functioning has turned him into a frightful legend. Atticus, ever stoic and loving, teaches his children about kindness and respect for others through his own actions, such as accepting hickory nuts as payment for legal services.

One day, the town judge comes to Atticus's home to ask Atticus to defend Tom Robinson (Brock Peters), a black man accused of raping a white woman. Being the most respected man in town isn't going to prevent Atticus from feeling the wrath of many of the town's intolerant citizens, who aim on lynching Tom Robinson. A famous northern lawyer felt the same scorn a century earlier when he, John Adams, was the only lawyer in Boston willing to represent six British soldiers accused of murder in 1770 for what became known as the Boston Massacre. Whereas Adams succeeded in his trial, Atticus does not, but not for lack of strategy and eloquence. The courtroom scenes—particularly Atticus's closing argument—are compelling, but the jury disregards the evidence, or lack thereof, against this unjustly accused defendant. This is a majestic film, tragic and uplifting.

Key Scene—The scuttlebutt about Atticus Finch's willing representation of a black man accused of raping a white woman reaches Scout. She gets into a fight with a boy at school who said her daddy defends n-----s. Scout asks her father why he is defending Tom Robinson, and Atticus explains to her that it is his duty to represent Tom, that if he didn't, he couldn't hold his head up in town.

Discussion Suggestion—Considering the criticism and anger many criminal defense lawyers receive for taking the cases of "known criminals," this scene could be used as a starting point to discuss if and when a defense lawyer should refuse a case, or should be criticized for taking a case.

Key Scene—The key witness examinations would be best shown together, even though they are lengthy. Robert Ewell, the alleged victim's father, testifies about seeing Tom attacking his daughter. He is then cross-examined by Atticus, which includes establishing that Ewell is left-handed. Atticus is attempting to show that Ewell beat his daughter, and Tom didn't. Then, Mayella Ewell testifies about how Tom raped her in her house. Atticus catches Mayella in lies, which causes her to come unglued. Atticus takes some evidentiary liberties to show that Tom couldn't have beaten her as her bruises indicated since he has the use of only one arm. Then, Tom takes the stand and tells the jury how he—like the Old Testament's Joseph with Potiphar's wife—was trapped by Mayella and that she kissed him against his will. At that point, Mayella's father came into the house and Tom ran off. Tom is then cross-examined by the prosecution.

Discussion Suggestion—Considering the charge was rape, where was the evidence of it? Was there any evidence of sexual contact, much less rape? Should Atticus have moved for a directed verdict before even putting Tom on the stand? What, in your jurisdiction, is sufficient in order to convict someone of rape?

THE VERDICT (R; 1982)

Key Themes: Medical malpractice, civil litigation, David versus Goliath, redemption
Best Classroom Use: Civil Procedure, Litigation, Torts, Legal Ethics, Introduction to Paralegal Studies

122 minutes   (strong language, domestic violence)
Cast: Paul Newman, Charlotte Rampling, Jack Warden, James Mason

Here is a movie that may be hard to find, but is well worth the search. Before *The Rainmaker* and *A Civil Action*, there was *The Verdict*, a thoroughly absorbing film about a forlorn lawyer against the system, representing a powerless client against a powerful law firm and its omnipotent client. Five Oscar nominations were awarded to *The Verdict,* including Best Picture, Best Actor for Paul Newman, and Best Supporting Actor for James Mason, who plays the lead defense attorney. Although criticized by some lawyers at the time of it release for being unfairly unrealistic, this movie truly succeeds at being a magnificent legal drama.

Paul Newman plays Frank Galvin, a pathetic, alcoholic, nearly disbarred lawyer who goes to funerals handing his business card to the bereaved. Why Galvin was nearly disbarred helps to explain the alcoholism, which helps to explain why he only has one client, a young woman left brain-dead after general anesthesia was administered to her while in a Catholic hospital in Boston. Galvin's only friend and mentor (Jack Warden) gave Galvin the case because it is such a clear candidate for settling, and might help Galvin get back on his feet. Galvin has ignored the case for 18 months, and it is headed for trial soon, so he hurriedly talks up the prospects of a settlement while meeting with the woman's guardian, her sister. But while taking Polaroid pictures of his client in her bed in the hospital ward to use in his settlement conference with the Boston archdiocese, Galvin sees his only chance for redemption in those photos. He refuses the $210,000 offer and then begs his only friend to help him get this case ready for trial in two weeks.

Opposing Galvin is the brilliant and silky Ed Concannon (James Mason), the senior partner of a large defense firm who will stop at nothing to win his case, including using a spy against Galvin. As Concannon prepares the anesthesiologist for the witness stand and gets the press to write a few feel-good stories about the doctor, Galvin is struggling to find his expert witness, who had earlier agreed to testify that the hospital's employees were negligent. Since his client's heart stopped for nine minutes after aspirating in her general anesthesia mask, Galvin needs to show that the doctors' choice of general anesthesia was wrong. If, as the young woman's sister had told Galvin, she had eaten soon before entering the hospital, then the anesthesiologist would clearly have been negligent to use the general anesthesia. But the admission documents state the woman had eaten nine hours earlier. As Galvin labors to get hostile nurses who were on the scene that day to agree to help him, he loses his key witness, who was bought off by the defense. The trial judge, neatly in the defense's back pocket, refuses to grant Galvin an extension, scolding Galvin about his foolish refusal of the Catholic Church's offer.

At trial, Galvin's replacement expert witness doesn't exactly instill awe, especially after the judge takes over the examination. And there is still the matter of the missing admitting nurse, who Galvin is desperately trying to find in the middle of a trial being handled so deftly by his opponent. While it is easy to notice the dirty tricks pulled by the defense lawyer, one must also realize that Galvin could be sanctioned for the many ethics violations he commits: miscommunication with the client's guardian regarding a settlement offer, wrongful solicitations, lying, deceit with unrepresented persons, and more. Then again, saints don't need redemption.

Key Scene—The movie opens with a short sequence of Frank Galvin paying his way into funerals so he can approach the widows to lie to them about having being friends with the dead, and then present his business card. Eventually, he is caught and thrown out.

Discussion Suggestion—Although it might seem obvious, you could discuss what specifically was unethical with Galvin's solicitations. That it occurred at funeral homes showed it to be despicable, but that alone isn't what made it wrong.

Key Scene—After taking the Polaroid pictures of his client, Galvin meets with Boston's archbishop, who offers $210,000 to settle the case, a number Galvin realizes is easily divisible by three. Refusing to take such an easy contingency fee, Galvin states that if he took the money, he would just be a rich ambulance chaser. Leaving the meeting, Galvin goes to see the friend who threw him the case years earlier, and begs for his help in the trial preparation.

Discussion Suggestion—Although noble, was Galvin correct in refusing such a settlement? Who has the authority to accept or reject settlement offers?

Key Scene—Attorney Concannon meets with his staff in a regal boardroom and plots a strategy for the upcoming trial now that Galvin rejected the settlement offer. Galvin's history of personal difficulties becomes a point of discussion. Concannon orders the review of every deposition and other file documents, mentioning that the depositions seem to show that the plaintiff hadn't eaten for nine hours before being admitted to the hospital. Concannon also suggests that someone should get the Boston press to run some favorable stories on one of his clients, the anesthesiologist.

Discussion Suggestion—If you haven't watched the movie up to this point, use this review to provide a short summary in order to start a discussion on what the plaintiff would need to show to prove medical malpractice, and what the defense would need to do to rebut the claim. What types of evidence would either side need to find in order to support their cases? What types of tasks might paralegals engage in if working for either side?

Key Scene—After Galvin steals a phone bill to find the whereabouts of the missing admitting nurse who might, and does, know that the plaintiff had eaten within one hour before coming to the hospital (not nine hours, as claimed by the defense), he brings the nurse to testify. On cross-examination, she is asked why she would lie about when the plaintiff had last eaten, since she put a "9" on the admitting documents. She says she didn't, but that the anesthesiologist coerced her to change the "1" to a "9" after the fact, once the doctor realized he had been too tired that day to carefully pay attention to the admitting documents. Stunning the defense, she testifies that she made a copy of the original document, before changing it. Concannon questions her a bit more and then asks the judge to disallow the document she brought, arguing that it is inadmissible as a copy since the original is available. The judge agrees, over Galvin's objection. Concannon then asks the judge to disallow all of the nurse's testimony since, as a rebuttal witness, she was there only to testify about the admitting document, which had just been ruled inadmissible. Once again, the judge agrees and orders the jury to disregard all of that witness's testimony.

Discussion Suggestion—Discuss the accuracy of the courtroom portrayal. Is there any way under the evidentiary rules that the nurse's copy, showing the fraud, could be admitted? Is she a rebuttal witness? If so, why would all of her testimony be disregarded? What about her testimony that the anesthesiologist threatened her into changing the document? Is that admissible hearsay?

WALL STREET (R; 1987)

Key Themes: Insider trading, business ethics, greed and redemption
Best Classroom Use: Business Law, Criminal Law, Legal Ethics, Introduction to Law

126 minutes   (profanity, nudity, sexual situations)
Cast: Michael Douglas, Charlie Sheen, Daryl Hannah, Martin Sheen, Terence Stamp, Hal Holbrook

Oliver Stone has made some of the more socially relevant and controversial movies of the 1980s and 1990s, including *Platoon*, *JFK*, and *Natural Born Killers*. Stone's films slant toward his politics, and *Wall Street*, a superb morality tale on insider trading and corporate raiders, is no different. Filmed before the 1987 stock market crash and released months after it, *Wall Street's* most famous phrase, "Greed, for lack of a better word, is good." is eerily close to what Ivan Boesky said in a commencement speech at the University of California-Berkeley in 1985. Michael Douglas's performance won him an Oscar for Best Actor, and Stone dedicated the film to his father, who was a stockbroker. Students will love this movie and will be eager to discuss insider trading, corporate malfeasance, and of course, the pros and cons of greed.

Charlie Sheen plays Bud Fox, a young stockbroker spending his days sitting in a row with other cold callers who are trying every angle to make a stock sale. One of the calls Bud has made for 58 days in a row is to the office of Gordon Gekko (Michael Douglas), attempting to get a meeting with the investing maverick. On the 59th day, Bud gets his wish and finds himself in the cavernously luxurious office of the titan of other people's industry. Underwhelmed by Bud's stock recommendations, Gekko tells Bud, "Tell me something I don't know." And the hook is set. Bud mentions to Gekko that Blue Star Airlines has received a favorable judgment in an airline crash suit, which even the plaintiffs have yet to learn. Bud knows this inside information because his father (Martin Sheen) is the head of the mechanics union at Blue Star. Amused by Bud's moxie, Gekko gives Bud money to buy some shares in Blue Star and a few other companies.

Such a hit can only last so long and Bud is soon losing money in Gekko's account on stocks whose purchases were the result of traditional research. At a later gathering in Gekko's limo, Gekko once again uses insult to entice Bud by telling Bud that if he wants another chance with Gekko, he should stop "sending" him information, and start "getting" him information. To Bud's protests about the risk of losing his broker's license, Gekko responds, "If you're not inside, you're outside." And from there, Bud sets about gathering information on the next move of Gekko's nemesis, Sir Laurence Wildman, who has made even more money than Gekko from buying up the shares of depressed companies and then selling them off in pieces, killing thousands of jobs in the process. As Bud becomes richer, he becomes less circumspect about his activities, even visiting an old college pal who is an attorney in a corporate law firm and asking for inside information from the from the client files. When that doesn't work, he gets a night job as a custodian and begins stealing the information from the filing cabinets.

Bud still craves legitimacy and convinces Gekko that a friendly takeover of Blue Star Airlines would be a great investment, provided the company's unions will give some temporary concessions. Bud's father realizes what is going on, that they are all pawns of Gekko, and expresses in no uncertain terms his opposition to Gekko's involvement in Blue Star. Bud naively believes he will be installed as Blue Star's president to help turn the company around, but soon stumbles into the realization that Gekko was, all along, secretly planning to sell Blue Star in as many parts as possible. Bud's earlier illegal stock trades have caught the attention of the SEC, and after succeeding in getting his revenge on Gekko (with the help of Laurence Wildman), Bud is finally arrested for insider trading. To garner a little sympathy at his sentencing, all that is left for Bud is to help his accusers hook the bigger fish.

Key Scene—At the first meeting between Bud and Gekko, Bud tries to impress his hero with a box of Cuban cigars and stock recommendations. But Gekko is more interested in checking his blood pressure. This scene is demonstrative of how power begets information, as we watch Gekko surrounded by the trappings of immense wealth, dressed and coiffed impeccably, reacting unenthusiastically to all of Bud's stock picks, calling them dogs. Bud is losing his only shot to make an impression, so he finally blurts out Blue Star Airlines, disclosing the inside information on the favorable court ruling and how he learned it.

Discussion Suggestion—Upon viewing this scene, discuss what exactly is inside information, and when does acting upon it constitute illegal insider trading. Is it based on the tipper/tippee or misappropriation theories of liability?

Key Scene—Starting to feel his oats after being beguiled by the trappings of his ill-gotten gain, Bud heads to the law office of an old college pal (James Spader), digging for inside information about the firm's corporate clients. Eventually, Spader agrees to park stock trades for Bud after being told it's the easiest money he can make.

Discussion Suggestion—Has James Spader's character done anything illegal? Has he done anything unethical? If so, what?

Key Scene—The most famous line of the movie—"Greed, for lack of a better word, is good"—has been glibly pilloried, when in fact the context for Gekko's statement shows him to be historically and prophetically correct. Speaking at the Teldar Paper shareholders meeting, as a renegade shareholder trying to wrest control of the company from the board, Gekko makes one of the best arguments for shareholders rights this side of the 2008 and 2009 stock market and credit meltdowns.

Discussion Suggestion—This scene could be debated for hours, discussing whether greed does "clarify." As Gekko prosecutes the board and executives for their lack of personal stake in Teldar and highlights its bloated state, including employing over 30 vice presidents, is Oliver Stone, perhaps unintentionally, making the case for entrepreneurial driven capitalism and a return to respect for shareholders?

THE WAR OF THE ROSES (R; 1989)

Key Themes: Divorce and property distribution, spousal conflict
Best Classroom Use: Family Law, Alternative Dispute Resolution

116 minutes   (violence, strong language)
Cast: Michael Douglas, Kathleen Turner, Danny DeVito

As portrayed in *The War of the Roses*, a marriage doesn't break like a bone; it decays like a tooth, slowly reaching a point of ruination. And it is at this point that this film serves up as a black comedy feast. Some Family Law students might even see parts of themselves or their clients in *The War of the Roses*.

Oliver and Barbara Rose meet in Nantucket, as young and idyllic scholarship Ivy Leaguers. Oliver (Michael Douglas) is going to Harvard Law, and in a whirlwind romance, they soon become newlyweds, have twins, and live in an upstairs apartment while Oliver strives to make partner. At a dinner party they throw for his partners, we start to see the tensions underneath their shiny veneer as Oliver asks Barbara (Kathleen Turner) to tell a story. Annoyed by how long it takes her to tell the tale of the purchase of their crystal glasses, he interrupts her repeatedly and finally just finishes the story for her. Eventually, they get the house of her dreams, an old mansion in need of refurbishing—which she does with his money—as he has made partner, working round the clock.

Years pass and she starts a catering business. They drift apart, and after Oliver suffers a heart attack scare one night, Barbara tells him that the thought of his demise made her feel free. She wants a divorce. He doesn't. But they both want the house and will stop at nothing to make sure that the other one doesn't get it. They first begin their fight over the house with offers: Barbara offers to give up any rights to alimony and his future income in exchange for the house. Oliver offers her almost $500,000 as payment for her prior marital services in exchange for the house. Barbara claims the house belongs to her because its stunning condition is due to all the efforts she alone put into it, which is true. Oliver claims the house belongs to him because he paid for it and all its improvements, which is also true. And, in a foreboding moment of rare clarity, Oliver's friend and lawyer, Gavin (Danny DeVito), cautions Oliver about his and Barbara's increasing insanity, telling him, "There is no winning in this, only degrees of losing."

The ever-escalating fight for the house heads to its inevitable conclusion, and we're left with the realization that two people truly did cut off their faces to spite their noses. Coincidentally, this movie bears an uncanny resemblance to the marriage of Andy and Martha Stewart—short of the deaths, of course. Andy was an Ivy League law student who met and married the poor but talented Martha, and their early years included throwing dinner parties in their apartment. They eventually found the perfect fixer-upper home in Connecticut and turned it into a showpiece, as Martha began a catering business and Andy helped her get a publishing deal for her first entertaining book. Their marriage ended after years of decay and part of their acrimonious divorce included a fight over their house, which Martha got.

In another coincidence, there is an ABC Primetime Live Special, "The War of the Roses," which concerns the astonishingly hurtful divorce between Michael and Rona Rose, two rich spouses fighting over their Miami home. The husband happens to be an attorney. This informative television show includes attempts to resolve their disputes with mediation. The show can be ordered from abcnewsstore.go.com.

Key Scene—After returning home from the hospital from having what he thought was a heart attack, Oliver confronts Barbara about her absence from his bedside. Eventually, she tells him how relieved she felt when she thought of him being dead. A few seconds later, she tells him she wants a divorce, and he angrily warns her, "You better get yourself a damned good lawyer." Soon after, Oliver and Barbara are sitting in Barbara's lawyer's office, where he tells Oliver of Barbara's demand of the house. To show Oliver how much more Barbara deserves the house than Oliver, Barbara's lawyer pulls out the deathbed note Oliver had written for Barbara, professing his love for her, and telling her how much he owes her for everything he has in his life. "You will never get the house!" Oliver snarls at Barbara, and after Oliver storms out of the office, Barbara's lawyer attempts to calm her nerves by calmly telling her, "By the time this is over, you'll think this is one of your lighter moments."

Discussion Suggestion—Upon watching these scenes, students could discuss whether what is in store for Oliver and Barbara Rose could have been avoided in mediation. Are there any interests represented by the spouses' mutually exclusive positions, which could lead to some alternatives that might result in a negotiated settlement?

Key Scene—Oliver and Gavin discuss the problem of Barbara's living in the house during the divorce, which Oliver fears might help her keep it. Gavin then tells Oliver of a law he found, designed for poor people who are getting divorced, which allows the parties to live in the marital home. So, Oliver moves back. Eventually, he offers Barbara about $500,000 for her share in the home, telling her he reached that figure by calculating her contribution to the marriage in the form of a salary and multiplying it by their years together. She refuses the offer. Not long after that, Oliver comes to Gavin's office with a blueprint of the house, showing how Oliver and Barbara have divided the house into zones for each of them. Somehow, Oliver thinks he's gotten the best of Barbara since his zones are larger than hers. Gavin then tells his friend and client, "There is no winning in this, only degrees of losing."

Discussion Suggestion—Discuss what factors go into determining who is awarded the marital home, and whether there is any disadvantage to the spouse who moves out of the home during the divorce. Discuss community property law and research your jurisdiction's approach to property distribution. On a broader note, you could kick around the meaning of Gavin's statement about degrees of losing. Divorced students might want to discuss how that statement applied to their divorces.

THE WINSLOW BOY (G;1999)

Key Themes: Justice, litigation risks
Best Classroom Use: Interviewing, Introduction to Paralegal Studies

104 minutes
Cast: Nigel Hawthorne, Rebecca Pidgeon, Jeremy Northam, Gemma Jones

Set in London around 1912, *The Winslow Boy* (originally a play based on an actual case) concerns a well-to-do banker's family with three children: a self-proclaimed feminist fighting for women's suffrage, who wears men's ties and smokes cigarettes; an older son at Oxford; and a younger son of about 13 who attends a military boarding school typical of that high station in life. While the family is hosting a Sunday dinner with the daughter's fiancé, younger son Ronnie returns home unannounced looking worried, carrying a letter announcing his expulsion from the military academy for forging and cashing another student's money order. The father (Nigel Hawthorne) believes his son's simple denial of the charges, and sets about trying to get justice for Ronnie.

Because this is technically a military legal matter, there is almost nothing the family can do. But the father keeps spending his family's fortune on lawyers, and is finally granted a meeting with Sir Robert Morton (Jeremy Northam), the best lawyer of that era. Sir Robert, as he's called, meets with the boy and interviews him regarding the forgery and theft accusations, concludes the boy is telling the truth, and tries to get a trial. The problem is, because the boy was attending a military school, there is almost no opportunity to appeal the guilty determination except through a petition by right, which is a direct plea to the Attorney General to grant an appeal more on equitable than legal grounds. As Sir Robert attends the House of Commons trying to get his appeal granted, the father's health is weakening, the family's fortunes and reputation are dwindling, and the daughter's engagement is breaking up because the fiancé's family is embarrassed by all the negative publicity this cause celebre is receiving.

Due to a moving speech in the House of Commons, the petition by right is granted, and a trial takes place. Throughout it all, the family tries to remain unified, even as the mother questions whether this ruinous fight is worth it all. Taking place off camera, the trial is referenced through the conversations of the family members and Sir Robert. And, thanks to Sir Robert's brilliant cross-examination of the Crown's handwriting expert, the Attorney General drops the case before its conclusion, and the boy's innocence is declared. Surprisingly, the boy, for whom the family gave up its social standing and wealth, is nonplussed by the outcome, but the movie is more about a father's stubborn willingness to risk all in order to right a wrong.

Key Scene—At the first meeting between Sir Robert Morton and the Winslows, Sir Robert interviews the boy. Interrogation might be the more appropriate term, because it is a harsh and accusatory examination of the boy's version of events, focusing on time and place details. The examination is masterful, with many insightful particularization and probe questions. To the family's surprise, Sir Robert declares the boy innocent and takes his case. A few scenes later, Kathryn asks Sir Robert why he believed in the boy's innocence. Sir Robert explains the key aspects of his interview: The boy made too many damaging admissions that a guilty person wouldn't make, and when faced with an easy excuse for the crime (that the boy was just playing a prank and didn't intend to steal the money), he didn't take the bait, which was more proof of his believability.

Discussion Suggestion—One could gain a lot from these two scenes, particularly if upon watching the first scene, one would consider why Sir Robert declared the boy innocent. Then, after watching the second scene, it would be interesting to see how well the thought pattern matched Sir Robert's. From an interviewing perspective, think about how follow-up questions require a clear head, preparation for the interview, and good listening skills.

On a broader level, the viewing of this film could lead to a discussion about the advantages and disadvantages of alternative dispute resolution to traditional litigation. Although ADR wouldn't have been eligible for such a case as presented in *The Winslow Boy*, there are still applicable issues to consider: the costs, publicity, and stresses involved in traditional litigation.

YOUNG MR. LINCOLN (G; 1939)

Key Themes: Justice, wrongful accusation, courtroom shrewdness
Best Classroom Use: Criminal Procedure, Criminal Law, Interviewing, Alternative Dispute Resolution

100 minutes
Cast: Henry Fonda, Alice Brady, Marjorie Weaver, Arleen Whelan

Perhaps no one in American history is more revered than Abraham Lincoln. Thrust from relative anonymity and lukewarm support into the White House during America's most trying time, reviled for much of his presidency, then martyred at the dawn of peace, Lincoln's shadow has never waned. And through all the political failures Lincoln endured prior to the 1860 election, Lincoln's greatness as an Illinois attorney was never in doubt. *Young Mr. Lincoln* is a love letter of a film, more hagiography than biography, but the essence of the film, which is that Lincoln was both a good person and a good lawyer, rings true.

Moving through a 10-year time period in which Lincoln loses his beloved Ann Rutledge and becomes a lawyer (thanks to being given a set of Blackstone's *Commentaries*). The cardinal focus in *Young Mr. Lincoln* is on a famous criminal trial believed by a few Lincolnphiles never to have occurred, in which Lincoln, wonderfully played by Henry Fonda, defends two brothers accused of murdering a town bully late on the night of a town fair. According to the contemporaneous accounts, Lincoln defended one man, not two brothers, wrongfully accused of murder, late in Lincoln's legal career, not early in it. The movie's inclusion of Stephen Douglas as a possible suitor to a young Mary Todd is cheesy, and the trial scenes are presented with Hollywood histrionics, but they still are priceless examples of Lincoln's razor sharp wit and shrewd legal mind.

Key Scene— Early in the film, after Lincoln has set up his new law practice with another lawyer, two farmers come to see Lincoln about their lawsuit. It seems that the one farmer beat up the other because of unpaid debts and other alleged contract breaches. As Lincoln reads the personal injury complaint aloud, the farmers agree that's what happened. Then Lincoln reads the complaint for damages on the unpaid bills, and the farmers agree on the facts again. Lincoln notes that one farmer is suing the other for $250, while the other is suing for $245 and change. Smoothly, Lincoln tells them that their lawsuits cancel each other out, with a $4 difference, which he'll take as his fee for helping them settle their dispute. And in a matter of minutes, a lawsuit has concluded.

Discussion Suggestion—This scene could be shown in conjunction with a discussion of Alternative Dispute Resolution, because it neatly displays some of the primary advantages of ADR. Although each farmer believes they must have their day in court, Lincoln, acting almost as an aggressive mediator, helps them to see why settling makes much more sense.

Key Scene—The truly great portion of the film, and the scene which has reached legendary status, is late in the film where Lincoln cross-examines the key witness to the murder, who has heretofore sealed the defendants' fate. The witness testifies that he saw the murder, even though it was late at night and far from any lantern. Lincoln perfectly paints him into a corner, questioning the man repeatedly about how he could have witnessed something like that in the dark. The man then asserts that the moonlight that night helped him see the whole affair, to which Lincoln produces a farmer's almanac, showing that on the night in question the moon wasn't out that late. After catching the witness in the trap, Lincoln then declares the man the murderer, and off to jail the witness goes, as the brothers are freed.

Discussion Suggestion—After watching this scene, discuss how strong listening skills and sharp follow-up questions helped Lincoln save the day. The ability to ask good particularization and probe questions are essential to being a good interviewer, and this scene could lead to an interviewing role play, hopefully less aggressive than Lincoln's cross-examination.